GOLD TOWN TO GHOST TOWN

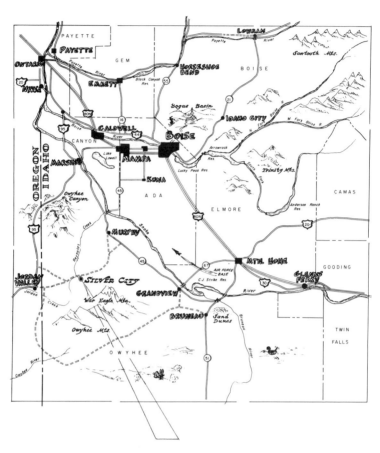

SILVER CITY

VICINITY MAP

Map 1

Gold Town to Ghost Town
The Story of Silver City, Idaho

Julia Conway Welch

University of Idaho Press
Moscow, Idaho

UNIVERSITY OF IDAHO PRESS
Moscow, Idaho 83843
First published in 1982 by the University Press of Idaho.
Printed in the United States of America
93   5   4   3

Library of Congress Card Number 82-60053

I S B N 0-89301-087-1

To
James C. Welch
1911 — 1978

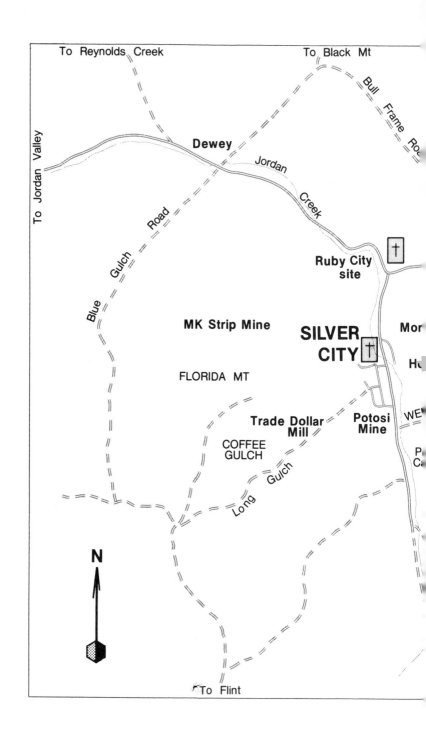

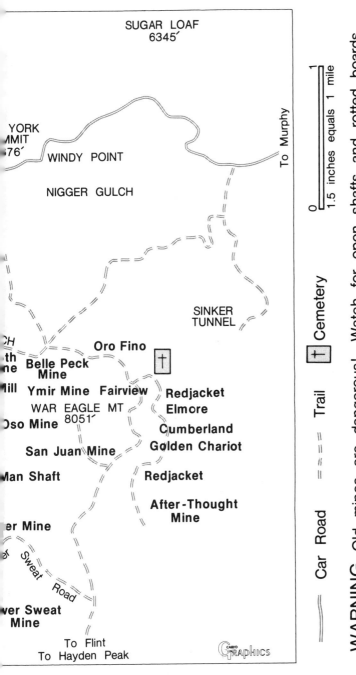

SUGAR LOAF
6345′

YORK
MIT
76′
WINDY POINT

NIGGER GULCH

To Murphy

SINKER
TUNNEL

CH
th
ne Belle Peck
Mine Oro Fino

ill Ymir Mine Fairview Redjacket

WAR EAGLE MT Elmore
Oso Mine 8051′

San Juan Mine Cumberland
Golden Chariot

Man Shaft Redjacket

After-Thought
Mine

er Mine

Sweat Road

ver Sweat
Mine

To Flint
To Hayden Peak

0   1
1.5 inches equals 1 mile

✝ Cemetery

Car Road = = = Trail ✝ Cemetery

WARNING Old mines are dangerous! Watch for open shafts and rotted boards.

Owyhee County Historical Society

Source: P.G. Anstey 1966

CARTO GRAPHICS

ACKNOWLEDGMENTS

I would like to thank the following individuals for their help in the production of this book: my sister Ellen J. Loney for helping with some of the research; my cousin Frances Feuling for saving clippings about Owyhee County during the years when I was out of the state; my niece Louise Eddy for typing the final manuscript; Arthur A. Hart for reading and commenting on the first writing of it; Elaine Leppert of the Caldwell Public library for running down books and articles for me.

I would also like to thank the following institutions for providing materials: the Wisconsin Historical Society for providing microfilm and film prints from the *Owyhee* (and *Idaho*) *Avalanche;* the Idaho Historical Society for supplying books and some of the pictures which appear in the book; the Owyhee Historical Society for information and pictures; the Owyhee County Courthouse for giving me access to files of pre-trial hearings and for other necessary information; the Bureau of Land Management for the use of their Environmental Impact Study and other courtesies; the Medford Public Library of Medford, Oregon; the Jackson County Historical Society for the opportunity to view microfilm of the *Oregon Sentinel* and the *Jacksonville Sentinel;* the Caldwell, Idaho Public Library; and the Idaho State Historical Library.

Julia Conway Welch

The single-page maps in the book are either copied directly or modified from those in the Bureau of Land Management's Draft Environmental Impact statement with the permission of the BLM. The double-page map is based on those supplied by the Owyhee Historical Society.

INTRODUCTION

We used an expression in the town I grew up in which characterized our geographical location — a gulch in some high mountains rising out of the desert in a sparsely populated corner of the West. When we were going out of town we would say we were going to the "Outside." And if we saw a stranger in town we would say that he or she must be someone from the "Outside." Prisoners use the same expression and we likewise felt cut off from the rest of the world, prisoners of heavy snow in winter and the rough nature of our roads in all seasons. That word also described what we saw from the summits of our mountains whose seven and eight thousand foot altitudes provided an eagle's eye-view of the country around us. Looking north and east we saw a vast panorama spread out like a relief map with steep mountains giving way to bare foothills and these to lava buttes along a winding river. Beyond there was another river with miniaturized towns along it and at night these patches of urban life twinkled with lights like reflected stars. Beyond the second river another range of mountains rose against the skyline. This awesome view of the Snake River Plain, the Boise Valley, and the Boise Mountains of Idaho was a sharp contrast to the narrow gulch we lived in where the sun was late reaching us of a morning and set all too soon over the opposite wall of mountain.

Looking south and west from the summits we saw the vast spaces of three states — Idaho, Oregon, and Nevada. Some accounts of the wonders of the view add California to the list but that may be stretching the limits of vision a bit. The deserts cut by pencil-line roads, the green valleys along creek beds, the many-forked Owyhee River, black lava formations, and the high mountains of eastern Oregon and northern Nevada make this view as wonderful as the other.

Our town was in a gorge cut by Jordan Creek in the Owyhee Mountains of southwestern Idaho. We called it "Silver", short for Silver City. The townsite was not the kind that would attract the eye of a city planner unless he was looking for a real challenge, for the steep sides of the gulch and the huge protruding rocks left few spots to build on. But this was the best of three sites tried along the creek for town building in the early days. Two earlier ones, Ruby City and Booneville, did not survive long enough to become ghost towns; their buildings were dismantled or in some cases simply moved intact up the creek to become part of Silver. The first settlements grew out of the rush of

Silver City (lower left) as seen from War Eagle Mountain, showing the surrounding rugged country.

placer miners to the area. Silver was closer to the rich quartz lodes, the source of the nuggets washed down the creek, and the discovery of their great wealth turned the excitement away from the creek and up to the mountain tops surrounding the town. After three years of life, Ruby City gave up the county seat to Silver in 1866 and many of its buildings were moved up the creek where some of them still stand.

These mountains are the outstanding feature of Owyhee County. The name "Owyhee," first given to the river that winds through the county and on into Oregon, is a variant spelling of Hawaii, the native home of three unlucky men who disappeared while trapping with a Canadian party along the stream in 1818. The county is the second largest in Idaho, and for its size the most sparsely populated. It had a population of 6,422 in 1970, which may have been about the size of Silver at its peak. By 1980 it had experienced a real boom for this part of the country by gaining 819 new residents. With its 7,841 square miles of land it provides close to one square mile per person. If such a size seems like plenty of elbow room it is nothing compared to the size of the original "County of Owyhee" as described by the Territorial Legislature of 1863. They gave it "all the territory South of the Snake River and West of the Rocky Mountains." This vast domain stretched across southern Idaho and on into Wyoming.

It is hard to believe that these mountains which stand out so sharply against the skyline within plain sight of the Oregon Trail were so long ignored, or at least so rarely mentioned by travelers. Peter Skene Ogden, the hardy Canadian trapper who left no stream untried in his search for beaver, penetrated the county along the Bruneau River in 1826-27. His opinion of the lowlands drained by the river which in those days was like most of southern Idaho — a vast sea of "wormwood" or sagebrush — was not kindly. "We certainly travelled over a barren country today," he writes in his Journal.[1] "Not even a bird or a track of an animal to be seen. 1 beaver this day." The next entry was even more bitter. "I verily believe," he writes. "A more wretched country Christian Indian or Brute ever travelled over or ever will...."

If he had followed the route of the present road from Murphy, Idaho which is now the county seat and the home of around fifty people, into the mountains, he would have found decidedly less wretched conditions about halfway along the twenty-three mile trip where the climate and topography change from desert to mountain in a matter of feet. This road winds up and down over treeless sagebrush hills, making seemingly aimless hairpin turns into one gully after another while the mountains ahead remain blue and distant. Finally it winds down a steep grade into the bed of a creek. The road goes up from here along another small creek called Sinker — a name which plays a part in the history and mythology of the region. The odor of sage and alkali dust and the high-pitched hum of insects accompanies you as you follow the little creek until the cottonwood trees begin to give way to junipers and mountain mahogany whose spicy fragrance drifts in on the sudden cool breath of mountain air. As you turn away from the little creek, you have a glimpse of War Eagle Mountain on your left, massive and close. Your car may have told you that you have been climbing steadily since you left the creek bed and it may not be good news that you are about to begin the long climb to the summit. Modern cars sometimes overheat on this road, but not like they did in the early part of the century when drivers sometimes had to back down after stalling and add water to boiling radiators. The road turns and climbs into the heart of the mountains whose steep sides drop down into gulches beyond the reach of the eye. Rocks are huge, and among them the pointed alpine fir and gently rustling aspen and a profusion of wild flowers add color and variety to the slopes. A turn in the road leads into the sudden dense shade of firs. Snow lies a long time in this spot keeping the road closed after the rest of it is bare. Out of the shade you come into the dazzling light of barren New York Summit and looking back from it you can see the whole "Outside." The scene is not so wonderful today as it was fifty years ago when on a clear day you could see the capitol building and the railroad station in Boise seventy miles away. Now the polluted air from too many cars hangs like a shroud over Boise Valley. If you turn and look the other way you see the mine-scarred back of Florida Mountain, the scene of the second boom which brought the town new prosperity in the '80s, '90s and early 20th century just as War Eagle brought its first boom in the '60s and '70s. The town is hidden until you reach the bottom of the summit close to the banks of Jordan Creek. Silver will come into view as you take the road to the left. If you took the road to the right you would come to the spot five miles down the creek where gold was first discovered in 1863 and where the life of this whole region began.

1

The discovery of gold at Sutter's mill in California in 1848 inspired a lot of people to try creeks and rivers all over the West for placer gold. Idaho was invaded from the south and west by prospectors who had arrived too late to stake a claim at some other diggings. The gold in Jordan Creek was not discovered until 1863, three years after the first discovery of gold at Pierce in the Idaho panhandle, and after miners were already washing out nuggets in the creeks of Boise Basin less than a hundred miles away.

Rumors of gold in the Owyhees preceded the discovery and a tantalizing story which came to be known as the Blue Bucket Legend made every untried stream a possible bonanza site. The legend is told in different ways with many ingenious additions. Emigrants on their way to Oregon, the legend had it, found nuggets in a creek which they used for sinkers on their fishing lines, tossing them into a blue bucket in their wagon to use again. They were seen after the party arrived in Oregon by someone who recognized them as gold, but by that time the emigrants had crossed many creeks and the True Creek became as elusive as the Holy Grail.

A man who developed some of the first rich quartz mines in the Owyhees claimed (some thirty-five years later) that the legend inspired him to prospect along Sinker Creek in Owyhee County a year before the discovery of gold in Jordan Creek. In an account he wrote of himself in 1898 he said that he tried the stream "upon the representation of a man who said he had a nephew who had been with a party on the creek in 1847 and that they had found gold so plentiful that they pounded it out on their wagon tires to make sinkers for their fish lines, thereby giving the creek its present name."[1] Whether the creek was named after this unusual type of fishing tackle or after the legend itself nobody now knows. Other sites in Idaho and many across Oregon have declared themselves to be the inspiration for the story. It has never been located to anyone's satisfaction and there are probably people today still looking for it.

Colonel (an honorary title bestowed on men who became rich in the West) D.H. Fogus was the man who said he prospected the stream. He had also been at Pierce when the first discoveries were made there, and he had gone with the rush to Florence, Idaho and to Powder and Burnt River, Oregon strikes. He must have at last made some money

J. Marion More (Idaho Historical Society).

when he landed in Boise Basin for when he came to the Owyhees from there he had enough capital to develop three promising mines and to build a toll road. His partner, J. Marion More, had done well there, too, and the two men used some of their profits to bring the first ten-stamp mill to the mountains. It was a gamble. The machinery itself was expensive and getting it into a country without roads was even more so. But the gamble paid off and they recovered almost a million dollars in their first year. After that, trouble, partly of their own making and partly because of the costs of mining in this isolated spot, forced them to give up their best mines to a cooperative of miners in payment of debts. But they recovered from that reverse in time to be in on the second big strike on War Eagle Mountain and to take part in a shooting war there — the second one between mining companies who claimed that miners on the other side were taking ore from veins on their property. Fogus' partner, J. Marion More, was shot and killed in front of the Idaho Hotel in Silver in 1868 when he exchanged insults with a man who favored the other side.

Fogus may have panned the first gold in the county but he evidently did not find enough to get excited about. Another party in Boise Basin became disillusioned with prospects there and retraced its steps west to the Owyhees where they found plenty of excitement on the banks of Jordan Creek which they named in honor of their leader Michael Jordan. Another member of the party, Oliver Purdy, wrote a lively account of the discovery twelve years later for the *Owyhee Avalanche,* Silver's newspaper, and the account appeared again in 1898 in a book published by the paper's editor.[2]

> We crossed the Snake River at the mouth of the Boise River, travelling in a southwesterly direction, until we came to, at that time, quite a large stream, which we named, in honor of the laziest man in the company, "Reynolds Creek." We camped here one day. During the day, two of the party, Wade and Miner, ascended the divide westerly from camp, on a tour of observation, and discovered still farther south and west what appeared to be a large stream, judging from the topographical formation of the mountains which were well timbered. This was reported to the balance of the camp.

> The next morning (May 18, 1863) our party of twenty nine men and about sixty horses and mules was headed in the direction of the supposed water-course, which we reached about 4:00 o'clock p.m., at a point we named "Discovery Bar" about six miles below where Booneville now is. The locality presenting a favorable place for camping, it was so agreed. Dr. Rudd, a verdant emigrant, not waiting to unpack his mule, took his shovel, and scooping up some of the loose gravel on the bank of the creek, panned it out and obtained about a hundred 'colors.' In ten minutes, every man, with pan and shovel (except the lazy man), was busy digging and panning, and upon their return about an hour after each man had favorable prospects to exhibit.

> The prospecting continued up the creek for ten or twelve days, when at "Happy Camp", the laws of the district were made and adopted, the creek and the district named and claims located — the creek and the district taking the names of two of our company, Michael Jordan and W.T. Carson.

Purdy's mention of formulating the law of the mining district was the accepted procedure for those who arrived first in a spot. It followed the tradition of prospectors in Nevada, California, and Oregon.

The book that carried Purdy's account in 1898 was published twenty years after his death. It is called *A Historical, Descriptive, and Commercial Directory of Owyhee County.* It was known in Silver as "The Blue Book" for its bright blue cover. Many households

A very early *Owyhee Avalanche* office (Owyhee Historical Society).

One of the first mills (1 mile south of Silver City), now gone (Owyhee Historical Society).

had a copy of it when I lived there and I remember one building which had a dusty stack of them in the corner. Today the book is a valuable historical item and a prized possession of those who were lucky enough to keep it. Although the tone of the book is generally promotional and some of its exclusions are more interesting than its inclusions, it preserved some history of the region. Like many other promotional ventures of its time it sold space in the last section for pictures and biographies of those who were willing to pay the fee. The biographies, often written by the subject himself, vary from simple straightforward accounts of the dates and places the person remembered to some rather grandiose accounts of what had been seen and done. In 1898, thirty-five years after the discovery of the gold in the creek, it was an honor, we gather from the book, to have been one of the first to be on the spot. D.H. Fogus claimed to have been among the first at six different spots. Another and perhaps an even greater honor was to have been an Indian fighter. Oliver Purdy lost his life playing a hero's part in the Battle of South Mountain, the last Indian skirmish in the county (June 7, 1878).

One account[3] claims that Purdy was the first to volunteer when a band of Indians invaded the ranch country of Owyhee County along the Snake and Bruneau Rivers and were thought to be threatening Silver City. The men intercepted the Indians near South Mountain, a peak in the Owyhees south of Silver and separated from it by Boulder Creek and a lava land mass. It is a spot far enough away to make one wonder if the Indians were not already headed for Oregon, a course they took right after the battle. South Mountain is very close to the Oregon border.

The Indians routed the volunteers who retreated to a nearby ranch. The next day the men recovered the bodies of Purdy and Chris Studer. Both were buried in Silver. One account of the incident points out that the Indians must have respected the bravery and daring of Purdy (his shot is said to have killed their leader, Buffalo Horn) because his body was not scalped and mutilated and his spurs were nailed to a bush. Ten years earlier his fellow discoverer Michael Jordan died at the hands of Indians not far from this spot and his body was horribly mutilated.

Perhaps the action of the volunteers averted a strike on Silver, but it is sad that part of the price paid for it was the death of Purdy. He was evidently a literate and intelligent man. He had taught one of the first schools in Silver, held county offices, and compiled a valuable record of the production of the early mines. If he had lived he could no doubt have written an interesting account of himself from the time he left Barre, New York for the California gold rush of '49.

13

Silver City, looking north in 1868 (Idaho Historical Society)

Silver City about 1870 (Owyhee Historical Society).

2

The discoverers panning out their first gravel along Jordan Creek didn't bother with a detailed description of their surroundings and it is easy to believe that they didn't spend much time communing with nature, with the possible exception of that lazy man Purdy spoke of. If he sat in the shade and watched his gold-crazed companions working up a sweat, he probably saw mountains, gulch, and creek very much as they are today. It is true that he wouldn't have seen the huge dumps of waste rock that mark the sites of the Dewey and Delamar mines. But even these are being invaded by tough mountain shrubs — rabbitbrush, sage, and juniper. If he had lived there after the mines started producing and after a stable population filled the gulch, he would have seen an entirely different topography. The "well-timbered" mountains Purdy spoke of were nearly denuded to supply the mines with wood for the first steam-powered machines, for buildings, and for fuel for the long cold winters. The Blue Book's directory for the towns of Silver, Blackjack, and Delamar lists forty-six men who cut and sold wood in 1898, an occupation second only to mining. And this was in a day when steam power for hoists and mills was out of date. When steam power was used, one mine on War Eagle Mountain contracted for one thousand cords of wood at a time to keep its boilers going. As the mines closed and the population shrank, the timber started coming back and with it deer and other wildlife returned, so that today, strangely enough, we see much the same scene the discoverers saw.

Two men who saw the beginnings of these towns along the creek approached it from opposite directions. Colonel (a true military title) C.S. Drew started from his home in Jacksonville, Oregon, another gold town whose rush began in the fifties shortly after the discoveries in California. He was carrying out a mission for the U.S. Army to map roads which could be used to protect travelers from Indian attacks. He left Oregon in 1865 with a party of thirty-nine enlisted men and with several migrating families under his care. It sounds odd to us now when we think of emigrants going from west to east, but that was the way much of early Idaho was settled. The tales of quick new riches attracted some; others came to find more living room in an unsettled country.

When he returned to Jacksonville, Drew published an account of his trip in the *Jacksonville Sentinel.* It was also published later as a

Ruby City, 1865 (Owyhee Historical Society).

pamphlet by the *Oregon Sentinel.* He called it "Owyhee Reconnaisance." His party forded the Owyhee River after crossing Oregon and entered the Owyhees along Jordan Creek. His route crossed the toll road already in operation from Booneville to Boise near Sucker Creek and he notes that families on ranches here have been staying with each other at night for fear of Indian attacks. He hears, too, about the deaths of Michael Jordan and others at the hands of Indians.

When he reaches the mountains he says of them that they are "well timbered with fir, pine, and a little of the cottonwood." Later on he says that the pine was not of good quality but it was used for lumber anyway. The fir trees came back after the drastic cuttings in the years that followed but the pine did not. Now the only specimens of pine near Silver are some scraggly growths which look like pinyon pine on some of the granite outcrops, for instance on top of Webfoot Rock, perhaps the biggest single granite boulder in the vicinity. The first lumber mill in the country, Drew says, brought down the price of lumber from three hundred dollars per thousand feet to half that.

Placer mining, which is confined to Jordan Creek, is the main oc-

16

cupation at this time, but quartz mining, Drew believes, will soon be the business of the region. Some of the placer miners recover as much as fifty dollars a day, "but the dust is of inferior quality, being alloyed with silver." He describes the gold and silver bearing lodes of Oro Fino Mountain (later named War Eagle) as being small "but exceedingly well defined," and he observes that four or five mills are nearly ready to start work.

His picture of the Owyhees is of a newly-opened country about to enter a period of frantic activity, a period marred by violence but nevertheless its liveliest and best. Just ten years after Drew saw it, it plunged into its first "bust." Booneville, Ruby City, and Silver which, with perhaps a touch of irony he called "the marts of commerce in that region", experienced a metamorphosis in 1875 which left Booneville and Ruby City empty and Silver a town of empty houses and idle mills. Ruby City at the time of his visit was still the county seat and it was connected with Boise by a route that brought daily postal service and "by pony express by way of Virginia City and Humboldt, Nevada, by which, in summer it is furnished with news only six days old." Soon the ponies were replaced by stage coaches and freight lines and the mines had an important link with the outside world.[1]

A visitor from the East, Albert D. Richardson, saw the Owyhee country in 1866. He was one of the most thorough chroniclers of the West. He tracked down everything that caught his eye from prairie dog holes to quartz mills. His book *Beyond the Mississippi,* published in 1867, covered much of the Midwest, the Southwest, California, Nevada, Colorado, Oregon, Utah, Montana, and part of Idaho. He had already covered the Pacific Coast states and gone on to Virginia City, Montana, when he decided to circle back and visit the famous Owyhees. His first impression of Idaho as he entered it from the east echoes what H.H. Bancroft later said about its effect on early travelers: "It was not regarded with favor by any class of men, even the most land-hungry." After a rough coach trip out of Montana Richardson wrote: "We were now in Idaho, barest and most desolate of all our Territories, with vast wastes of lava, sand, and sagebrush." He despairs of its future for agriculture (he should see what irrigation has done to it now) but extols its mineral wealth and the possible use of its "brown grass" for grazing. After a nine-day coach trip from Virginia City he arrived in Boise which he described as a "singularly beautiful frontier post" of two thousand inhabitants. However, he found Idaho society "not attractive." "Murders were frequent, for with a majority of industrious, law-abiding, settlers, the territory had also many late rebel soldiers; and the worst desperadoes from Califor-

Lithograph of Silver City, about 1865 (Owyhee Historical Society).

nia, Nevada, and Montana. The legislature contained just one Union member, and during the War there was more disloyalty than in any other northern Community except Utah."

His trip from Boise to the Owyhees was "over dreariest plains of sand and alkali, often too barren even for sage brush. For leagues on every side swept ashen treeless desert as sweeps the boundless seas."

Upon reaching the mountains he says: "Its metropolis is a straggling strip of town far up among the mountains, at one end called Booneville and at the other end Silver City, and in the middle Ruby City." The last he calls "a disorderly collection of buildings on a wooded hillside sloping down to Jordan Creek.......It is overlooked by summits of several mountains from 600 to 2000 feet above the town. Some are bare rock gashed with gorges and pointed turrets.......War Eagle is the king of all these peaks. Its crest is 5000 feet above the sea. (Its altitude is 8,065 feet.) It is the richest and most wonderful deposit of quartz in the United States, even eclipsing the Comstock lode."

His trip took place in a very wintry November but he was not deterred by the weather from seeing the famous mines at first hand. "In a biting wind that nearly swept us from our saddles," he wrote. "Our horses climbed the corkscrew road which winds up War Eagle Mountain." He "threaded the tunnel of the Oro Fino mine five hundred feet to its end where a shaft lets in daylight from 180 feet above." At the Poorman Mine he saw the famous Fort Baker which was built the year before during a dispute that nearly led to bloodshed over a rich vein of ore. He picked up a piece of native silver at this mine which he said was as big as a half dollar. And in spite of the bad weather he noticed the impressive view from the mountain top.

By 1866 eight mills had been built within the immediate vicinity of Silver; two, in fact, were in town. Two more were on the opposite side of War Eagle Mountain. Mining experts feel now that the lavish building of mills was a wasteful process because mining methods of the time were too primitive to supply enough rock to keep them running. Miners drove iron drills into the earth (much of it granite rock around Silver) and then filled the holes with black powder to blow the ground apart. The "muck" or waste rock from the explosions had to be carried to the surface from shafts by windlasses and buckets until steam hoists could be set up. Tunnels had to be cleared by wheelbarrow at first and then by muck cars on narrow tracks. Granite made for hard drilling which was slow, but soft ground called for timbering which was even more time-consuming. The work was hard and dangerous. A man who swung a "double jack" — the heavy hammer used to drive the drill — developed tremendous arm muscles and the pride he took

19

A drilling contest in the 1890s. The man with the stick will measure the depth of the holes (Idaho Historical Society).

in his work is illustrated by the fact that on holidays the drilling contest was the main part of the show. But many of these strong fellows ended up with a disease which was called "miner's consumption." We know now that it was silicosis contracted from inhaling the finely powdered rock from the drills. The early mines were unventilated except when it was practical to sink a shaft from above as Richardson mentions at the Oro Fino.

As if these hazards were not enough, the early developers often operated on the theory that the miners should be content to wait for their pay until the profits from the ore they took out rolled in. If the profits didn't materialize they were sometimes not paid at all; if the ore brought in handsome profits they got their wages and nothing more. This situation soon led to trouble for the operators. Other troubles plagued them, too, when disputes arose over claims which shared the same system of veins.

Pack mules in front of the Bibbins-Myer general store (Owyhee Historical Society). (early 1900's)

22

3

When the news of the Owyhee discoveries reached Boise Basin all kinds of hopeful people from incipient capitalists like Marion More and D.H. Fogus to poor men looking for work crossed the Snake River into the long-ignored mountains. Some of the men who had no money were lucky enough to stake claims which they sold to others who had, and these men built the roads and brought in the expensive machinery needed to separate the gold from the ore. They had the example of the California and Nevada mines to follow (especially the Comstock in Nevada where the situation was similar) and, although some simple extracting methods such as the arrastra — a turnstone which could be powered by a man, a mule, or a water wheel — were used, stamp mills were necessary for really big operations. These had to be located on a stream so that rock crushed by the stamps could be washed into settling tanks and over plates where the gold was picked up by mercury. The amalgam, that is, the metal combined with the mercury, had to go through a heating process in a smelter to free it from the quicksilver. It had to be sent out of the territory for the final smelting process in the early days.

Placer mining, though, was a game that even a poor man could play and make a considerable stake at, if he was lucky. He could get along with just a shovel and a gold pan and a creek that didn't dry up too soon, or he could buy a few boards and make a "rocker" — but he needed a partner to rock this simple box-like affair while he shoveled gravel into it. For a little more money he could make sluice boxes shaped like narrow open coffins with slats or riffles in the bottom. Mercury in the bottom of the riffles caught the gold as the miners shoveled in the gravel. But since it had taken uncounted years for the gold from the mountains to wash down into the creeks, placer gold was not, as we would say now, a renewable resource. And the water supply in these desert mountains was unreliable, too. Every gully would be roaring with water in the spring while the snow was melting and dry as a bone a few months later. So placer mining here as in other gold camps ended rather quickly until the patient Chinese came in to rework what the careless whites had left behind.

Because gold had been found first in central Idaho and in Boise Basin, there were established routes of transportation in operation by the time the Owyhee discoveries were made. Ships brought supplies up the Columbia River from the coast; first pack trains, then stage lines, brought them on from Umatilla, Oregon and Walla Walla, Washington. Soon the Owyhees were connected in another direction by way of Red Bluff and Chico. Supplies came up the California rivers from San Francisco; pack trains and wagons brought them on from there to the Owyhee River on the Oregon-Idaho boundary where they were ferried across and delivered to the mountains. Still later another route connected Boise and the Owyhees with the railroad at Kelton, Utah.

By the time goods arrived in Silver their price was inflated by transportation costs as well as by scarcity and demand. The Blue Book lists an interesting comparison of the prices of common articles in those days with those in the year of its publication (1898). Reading it today we can be doubly amazed at the high prices in 1867 and the low ones in 1897.

	1867	1897
Flour	$32.00 per hundred	$3.20 per hundred
Sugar	.60 per pound	.09 per pound
Coffee	.75 per pound	.18 per pound
Picks	$8.00 each	$1.00 each
Shovels	$4.00 each	$1.00 each
Heavy boot, miner's	$12.00	$3.00-$4.00
Hip gum boots	$16.00	$5.00

These high prices meant that money must be found to finance the mines — quantities of money. Most of the claims staked by early prospectors were sold to companies in the East and in California and Oregon, to Pennsylvanians, to New Yorkers, to Kentuckians, and to the British. Promoters took advantage of the fame of the early riches to sell stock in mines that didn't exist. People who got stung in this way spread the word and for a time even the mining journals were saying that the Owyhee region was a gigantic hoax. The next few years proved them very wrong: developers shipped over five million dollars worth of bullion from the region by 1869. Some of the ore was richer than the ore from the famous Comstock lode of Virginia City, Nevada. But the veins did not go deep into the mountains like the Comstock; they "pinched out" in miner's lingo, and this was a factor in Silver's early decline.

4

The ordinary miner who dug the valuable ore out of the mountains is often the forgotten man when the story of a town like Silver is told. There are other more glamorous items to stress — how rich the ore was, how many millions were taken out, how wild and rowdy the times were. One reason that the common man's story isn't told is, as Barbara Tuchman notes in *A Distant Mirror,* that day to day life doesn't leave a public record for historians to work with. The violent crime, the litigation over property, the money that changes hands, — all these things become part of history because they left a record. But we can surmise from some of the records that the miner's life in those times was far from easy. He was, no doubt, the victim of operators who hired him in hopes of digging into a rich vein and upon finding nothing left town before payday. This situation went on in many mining towns for years.

In 1867 in Silver, the miners met in the courthouse to form a union. After a brief strike, they won the right to be paid in bullion rather than the less valuable "greenbacks" and the right to be hired by contract. Wages were not an issue, for the Owyhee miners were paid five dollars a day, a sum that took into consideration the isolation of the mines and the subsequent high prices of common necessities, as well as the primitive accommodations provided. The Nevada mines were paying only two-fifty to three dollars at the time. But their victory in this case didn't mean that they were assured of steady work and pay. Mining was an up-and-down business for the operators, too. They over-expanded at times, as More and Fogus did when they lost out to a cooperative of miners. The price of metals and the state of mining stocks in California and the East made their chances of finding financial support dependent on a lot of factors outside the mining district. And the imprecise method of staking and defining claims led to clashes between mines that brought on disputes so severe that they sometimes ended in bloodshed. In one case mines on War Eagle were able to come to terms before any violent deaths occurred, although one mine built a fort and was ready to fight it out. Another one ended with the deaths of four men and the wounding of two and many shots fired underground where the miners worked.

The Poorman War (so called, for it was a war that didn't happen) of 1865 is a testament of the fact that some prospectors will go to any length of guile and trickery to get possession of valuable claims. A

Poorman Mine. On the slope left of center is the "fort" (Owyhee Historical Society).

man named Peck discovered a very rich body of ore close to a spot where a shaft was being sunk on the Hays and Ray Mine. The fact that he concealed his find and tried to buy the claims from the owners reveals that he must have known that the ledge was on their property. If he had gone to the men who were sinking the shaft at this point and told them about the find, there would have been no "war" and millions of dollars could have been saved. He made the mistake of leaving town, and other prospectors found his discovery. They staked claims which overlapped some of the rival claims and began taking ore from the valuable ledge. They justified their action by declaring that the rich vein was not the vein Hays and Ray were working on but an entirely new one parallel to it. They called their discovery "The Poorman", a name that might have been aimed at hiding the riches they knew were there. The Hays and Ray people knew they had to prove that this was not a new vein but the very one they were pursuing and they had to do it quickly before the vein was plundered by the Poorman miners. The company was too poor to hire a surveyor to trace it but by this time Peck had come back to town and was no doubt seething with chagrin. They hired him to trace it in exchange for an interest in their mine. While Peck traced, the Poorman men took out ore and before an injunction from the courts could stop them they managed to get away with half a million dollars from some of the most valuable gold and silver ore ever found on the mountain. When the news of this very rich ore reached Portland, a company which already had mining interests in the Owyhees — the Oregon Steam and Navigation Company which had made a fortune by transporting men up the Columbia to the mines — decided to back the Poorman in the legal battle they could see ahead. Fearing that mere money and lawyers might not prevail in the end they decided to use force. Armed men and a brush fire blocked Peck's path as he approached the Poorman claim. It looked as if a shooting war was about to break out, but the Hays and Ray people showed admirable restraint even when the other side built a log structure on their property which they called "Fort Baker" and made other warlike gestures. At this point another mining company on War Eagle decided to back Hays and Ray. They provided the money for an injuction and a judge arrived from Boise to hear the complaints. He did the only sensible thing which was to insist that the Poorman vein be uncovered in the direction of the other property. When this was done it was obvious that the vein led straight to the Hays and Ray claim. It looked as if a long court battle would now take place but lawyers for the two wealthy backers got together and reached an agreement. In the end they all profited hugely and even the original owners got something out of it. The ordinary miner working underground was probably thankful he didn't get shot. The judge who heard the complaints and made a wise decision was vilified by the name "Bribery Kelly" by those who thought the Poorman should have won it all.[1]

The second dispute took place in 1868 under similar circumstances but with graver consequences. The Golden Chariot and the Ida Elmore mines were working veins in the same system when it became apparent that they were "drifting" (tunneling underground) on a collision course. The two veins merged at a certain spot and this had been determined in time for the site to be declared neutral ground by both parties. D.H. Fogus and Marion More owned the Elmore and John Holgate operated the Chariot with another group. The trouble began when the Chariot men broke through the neutral zone. They were so close to the Elmore drift that the miners could hear each others' voices. The Elmore men protested the broken agreement, but seeing that their protests had no effect they armed their miners. The other side did the same and soon men were blasting away at each other underground. Both sides sent out of town for reinforcements — hired gunmen who made their living "settling" disputes in places where law-enforcement was non-existent. Some of the men may have been those Albert

27

Richardson referred to as "the worst kind of desperadoes" which he noticed in Boise. A lot of shooting took place underground but amazingly enough only two men were killed and one wounded. John Holgate of the Chariot side died from a bullet wound to the head on March 28, 1868. He is buried in the Pioneer Cemetery high on the mountainside east of Silver. His marble stone is one of five that have survived in that cemetery. It doesn't mention the conflict that brought about his death; it simply states "An Honest Man." The other man who died at the scene of the fighting was Meyer Frank who is identified in accounts of his death as "a Jew from Mobile, Alabama, who fought on the Confederate side in the Civil War." He was probably one of the imported gunmen, perhaps one of those "late Rebel Soldiers" Richardson spoke of. He was also buried among the many nameless in the same cemetery. Another man, James Howard, who fought on the Elmore side was wounded and recovered.

The Governor of Idaho Territory sent in a deputy marshal at this point with a proclamation ordering all parties to stop fighting and start talking. Surprisingly enough they reached an agreement with each side, as the *Owyhee Avalanche* put it "receiving enough to make them all millionaires." The newspaper also predicted that there would be "grand jollification in the town tonight."

The celebrating was probably still going on a week later when Marion More and Jack Fisher exchanged insults with Sam Lockhart who was sitting on the porch of the Idaho Hotel. The incident has been described as a drunken brawl but it probably would not have taken place if the bitter feelings over the recent "war" were not the prevailing sentiment in the town. When the shooting started More was struck in the chest. He ran a few feet and fell in front of the Chinese Restaurant where he was taken in and treated. He died the next afternoon. Jack Fisher was wounded in the thigh and Lockhart was severely wounded in the arm. Three months later Lockhart died in jail of blood poisoning after his arm was amputated by a doctor from Boise. T.S. Donaldson in his book *Idaho of Yesterday* says that the doctor received $2,500 in gold for the surgery. One of the remaining marble stones in the Pioneer cemetery is Lockhart's. More's body was taken to Idaho City in Boise Basin.[2]

The death of More was a shock to the Territory. He had been in Idaho since 1861 looking for prospects around the Elk City region in the central part of the State. He was one of the first to look for gold in the Salmon River country where he found encouraging pannings on Miller Creek which led to the birth of a small town — Millersburg — at an altitude of 8,000 feet. Bad weather forced abandonment of the town and news of the Boise Basin strikes drew More in that direction. He arrived at Centerville in the Boise Mountains in time to stake enough claims to give that town its first name, Hog'em — a tribute from those who came after More's party and found all the good claims staked. Idaho City was at first called More's Creek and the stream near there still bears his name. Early photographs of the leaders of the day include the well-dressed, bearded, handsome figure of More. If he had lived he would very likely have been one of the political or business leaders of Idaho. However he was not a popular figure in the Owyhees because of his failure to pay his workers and creditors when he and Fogus got into financial difficulties at the Morning Star and Oro Fino Mines.

After More's death Governor Ballard had the good sense to realize the seriousness of the situation. The Chariot-Elmore War seemed on the verge of breaking out again. He sent in troops — ninety-five men and a cannon — and kept the town under siege for five days. Tempers cooled and the men went back to work in the mines. After Lockhart's death all charges were dropped.

For the next seven years the mines on War Eagle Mountain continued to produce some of the richest ore found in the West. The Poorman, the Golden Chariot, the Ida Elmore, all won prizes at different times for rich samples of their ore. One batch from the Poorman weighing five hundred pounds was described as a "mass of ruby silver crystals." "Ruby" described the color of the ore which may have been proustite, a mineral that is rare in the United States. A portion of this crystal mass found at the Poorman won a gold medal at the Paris Exposition of 1866, carrying the reputation of the Owyhee Mines overseas.

A little town had grown up around these rich mines on the east side of War Eagle Mountain. It was called Fairview because the whole "outside" can be seen from it. During the '60s and '70s the town was a rival of Silver, even bidding for the county seat when Ruby City gave it up. But its 8,000 foot altitude and the blizzards that sweep that side of the mountain must have discouraged partisans of such a move. The town's history was brief. After a disastrous fire in 1875, it was not rebuilt. Today the hillside where all these violent struggles took place is bare of any structures. The mine dumps are still there but the people who could point out which mine was which are becoming fewer and fewer. There is a little cemetery on the lip of the hill below the old Oro Fino dump where a few marble stones commemorate some who are buried there. One of them tells a pathetic story. Thomas Thebo put it up in memory of his wife Mary Ann who had come to this remote mountain spot from her home in Nova Scotia. In her obituary notice in the *Avalanche,* Silver's newspaper, the writer says of her death from tetanus or "lock jaw" as it was called, "no pen can describe the tortures she suffered." She was thirty-two years old and the mother of four children. Her husband selected this verse for her gravestone which is sadly appropriate:

Dearest wife thou art gone to rest
Thy toils and care are o're
And sorrow -, pain, and suffering now
Shall ne'er distress thee more.

5

Although the War Eagle mines were sporadically troubled in the early '70s by labor disputes, money problems, poor equipment, and expensive transportation costs, many continued producing ore until 1875 when the Bank of California, a prime source of money for operating, closed its doors to prevent a run on its assets by depositors. In spite of the richness of the mines there was a gap between getting it out of the ground, milling it, sending it off to the smelters (one smelter in Swansea, Wales had the best recovery process for gold and silver and it was to the advantage of the operators to send it on that long journey to recover the maximum from their ore), and finally collecting its rewards. This gap had to be filled by banks and investors who could afford to spend large sums on the chance of making profits. It wasn't just the failure of that one bank in California that plunged Silver into a depression: it was the drying up of capital all over the country following the railroad building extravagances of the years before, their failure to turn a profit, and the disgraceful part members of Congress played in it by trying to feather their own nests. The panic of 1873 which followed destroyed confidence in any kind of investment and in the government itself.

There wasn't much a miner could do when he came to the end of a month and found himself without a payday and, often, a grocery bill at the general store. But one group of miners at that much-troubled mine, the Golden Chariot, gave it a try with an approach we would have to call "terrorism" today. They seized the superintendent, a Mr. Baldwin, whose promises of payday hadn't materialized and held him "in durance vile" to quote the Blue Book, until he made specific arrangements to go to San Francisco and return with a payroll to cover the missing wages. Baldwin was not harmed and he did return with the money. This incident is one of many examples of mines which closed without paying off its workers. In fact the practice went on through the years as long as mines were operating in the Owyhees — down to the thirties when reforms began. The Chariot closed along with the other mines on the mountain and the miners were not punished for their daring (and illegal) act. Many miners were stranded in town with their families and had to accept the charity of those who were more fortunate to survive. A prominent businessman, William Franz Sommercamp, is cited in his biography in the Blue Book for heading the

Colonel W.H. Dewey (Idaho Historical Society).

subscription list for the destitute in these hard times. We know that Mr. Sommercamp did not write his own eulogy for he died before the book was published of a tragic accident: he fell into a shaft while measuring a claim in 1890.

When it became evident that the situation wasn't going to improve quickly, over three hundred miners and their families left town. Some went to other mining camps. Some took up ranches in the valley. Some of the business people moved to Boise and other towns where they got in on the early bonanzas of urban growth — public utilities, hotels, and saloons. This was the first in a series of large exoduses in the boom and bust pattern of the mining town. Some die-hards stayed on and one who did not give up became the owner and developer of mines on the opposite wall of Silver — Florida Mountain — where a second boom proved greater than the first in total production. Its ores were "low grade" compared with the rich strikes on War Eagle, but the veins were wider and deeper. Improvements in both mining and milling made it possible to handle them now at a profit. The man who became a millionaire by developing and selling these mines was W.H. Dewey and he became famous in the region for more than the fortune he made. He was tried twice for the death of a man in a shooting scrape and his violent temper brought him into conflict with other men who were not exactly peace-loving either.

The mines on War Eagle opened again when the financial climate improved but the really big bonanzas had already been harvested up there. One by one the veins "pinched out." It was hard for the hopeful among prospectors and developers to believe that the really big stuff had given out. They went deeper into the mountain without any great success. The Poorman opened again and tried to revive its fortunes by cleaning out old veins, and looking for new ones. They built a new mill on Jordan Creek and installed a tramway to shoot the ore from the top of War Eagle to the mill. The London company who had bought the property must have put a fortune into the operation but the good old days of ore "richer than the Comstock" never came back.

Henry McDonald (Idaho Historical Society).

6

Two violent events in the '80s unconnected with mining operations made history in Silver. One of them in 1881 is written up in the Blue Book under the title "The First and Only Legal Hanging in Owyhee County." The other one concerned a very prominent man who was tried twice for killing a man in a gun battle. It is not mentioned anywhere in the Blue Book, not even in the biography of the man who was tried. The man who was hung was a stranger and also, I believe, a victim of what might be called "the Wild West Syndrome." Hangings had become a part of the folkways of the West, events that people traveled far to see and boasted afterwards of having witnessed. The way this hanging was written up in the Boise paper points to such a conclusion.

Henry McDonald was a teamster who worked out of Kelton, Utah at the north end of Salt Lake on the railroad. The body of the man he was accused of killing had been found in Owyhee County while McDonald was being held in jail in Boise awaiting the outcome of a grand jury investigation into the disappearance of George Myers, another teamster, whose outfit McDonald was in the process of buying.

In an interview with a reporter for the *Idaho Avalanche* (the same paper as the *Owyhee Avalanche*) three days before he was hung McDonald said: "I have always worked hard, and never done no harm; never had trouble with a man in my life except for a fight with High Rice at Kelton; he drew a knife on me, and I took it away from him and threw it away, because I didn't want to kill him. The people here are all against me, but where I have worked and am known, I don't believe they think I am so bad."

McDonald was a teamster who hired out to drive freight wagons from the railroad at Kelton, Utah to the Idaho mines. He was working for a Mr. Horne, carrying supplies to the Wood River and Hailey mines in Central Idaho when he met George Myers, an old teamster who wanted to sell his outfit in September, 1880. McDonald made a deal with him to buy it. He was to pay half the purchase price of $1,400 in cash and a hundred dollars a month on the balance until it was paid for, with the provision that the team was not to leave the Kelton road until it was all paid for. McDonald made arrangements to meet Myers at a station called Soul's Rest on the road after he had completed his last trip for Horne. Between Soul's Rest and Rattlesnake Creek,

35

Myers was killed and his body hidden not far from the road.

McDonald was caught in a tangle of false stories, forged letters, and attempts to implicate others. In the interview quoted above, three days before a death which he acknowledges as inevitable, he still insists that he had two confederates in the crime. One, a man named Lewis testified against him at the trial and denied any part in the murder. The other one McDonald named was Frank Kellet, a man who was never found. Was there a conspiracy among these men to kill and rob Myers with McDonald getting the team and the other two sharing the money McDonald had paid him? Evidently the jury in the trial didn't see much merit in the story, for they were out only an hour and five minutes when they found him guilty of murder in the first degree.

The reporter for the *Idaho Avalanche* agreed with the jury. "Thus," he writes, "ended an interview with one of the most cold blooded and brutal murderers that ever blackened the annals of crime." (This kind of superlative was typical of reporting in the West in those days) "During the entire talk the prisoner exhibited but little sign of emotion except when speaking of his wife and child and his mother. Then it was plain that he was making a powerful but ineffectual effort to control his voice and keep back the tears that would spring to his eyes. While telling of the brutal killing of Myers he exhibited no more emotion than a marble statue. He has told so many different stories, that people can place no confidence in this one, and it is probable that he would have told something else the next day."

At the trial McDonald claimed that the killing of Myers was accidental. He said that Myers was sleeping off a drinking bout in the wagon while he drove, that Myers' dog kept jumping out of the wagon and that he kept stopping to put him back in because he was tied in such a way that he had to keep walking on his hind legs to keep from choking. The frequent stops woke Myers and they quarreled about the dog, according to McDonald's story. The prosecutor maintained that McDonald had invented the story of the dog to make himself look like a man who couldn't bear to see suffering, as in the case of the dog.

In the course of the fight that followed, McDonald claimed that Myers made a move to get a gun from the "jockey-box" on the wagon. He was standing on the double-tree when McDonald hit him, causing him to fall and startling the team so that it ran and crushed him as he fell. At this point two men who had been riding with them earlier on horseback came along and persuaded McDonald to go on with the team, telling him that they would hide the body. These two men were Len Lewis and Frank Kellet. The motive McDonald assigned to them for being so obliging was that they knew the old man had the money McDonald had paid him on his person. Lewis denied all of this at the trial.

McDonald had changed his story by the time he talked to the *Avalanche* reporter three days before his death. He claimed then that the two men rode up while he and Myers were fighting and that after he hit Myers, Lewis clubbed him twice with a heavy stick and killed him. He said that he had not told this at the trial because he was afraid of Lewis.

The killing took place in September and McDonald was arrested in November and jailed in Boise on suspicion of murder when friends of Myers became concerned about his disappearance. McDonald told people that the old man had gone to Oregon with a group of immigrants he met on the road and he wrote letters signed with Myers name to keep up the pretense that he was still alive. In the Boise jail he fell victim to an old trick used by prosecutors to get evidence against a prisoner. It was the use of what McDonald called "a cat's paw" — a man placed in the cell who pretends to be friendly and helpful to the prisoner but is really eliciting information for the prosecutor. In this case a man named Gilnes encouraged, or according to McDonald inspired, him to write a letter to a friend in Kelton asking *him* to write a letter signed with Myers signature to keep up the pretense that Myers was still alive. It is hard to believe that anyone with very much intelligence would be persuaded to do such a thing, and McDonald said that he did not know that Gilnes had taken the letter with him when he left the cell. The next morning, he said, after he had thought it over he looked around the cell and couldn't find it. Gilnes, of course, had taken it to the prosecutor and it turned out to be a very incriminating piece of evidence for it showed not only his ruses for hiding information about Myers but identified his handwriting as that of the previous letters he claimed Myers had written. Up to this point he might have been freed because no body had been found to show that a murder had been committed, but the incriminating letter taken from his cell provided the grounds for holding him. In March, Myers body was found by Len Lewis' nephew. The identity of the finder makes one wonder if Lewis may have had a connection with the crime.

The trial took place in June, 1881 in the old courthouse on the east side of town which later burned. The defendant's statement, some of the witnesses' testimony, the prosecutor's and defense counsel's speeches, the judge's charge to the jury are all in the same issue. Some of the evidence is summarized rather than given in full. The October 15th issue of the paper contains the reporter's interview, the hanging story, and a letter from the man who was hung that day. In its brevities column a flippant note states that this is "black Friday" for McDonald. Another item gives credit to the man who built the scaffold.

McDonald's letter to the sheriff of Owyhee County appears under the title "An Open Letter" and the editor states that it was published at the request of the prosecutor, Tom Cahalan. The editor calls the letter an example of "unadulterated cheek," but by the time the paper came out McDonald was beyond the reach of any accusation of cheekiness or anything else. It is a bitter and vengeful letter, and the term gallows humor is all too appropriate:

"Mr. John Springer: [the sheriff]
Sir: you had better take that gallows and send it to Boise City, it may come in handy for the male hobbling bastards in that place. That will come handy for Gilnes [the cat's paw] or the man who got him to swear against me, Tom Cahalan, he may need some day to be hung and I would like to make them a present for the trouble I have put them too. It will help pay back some of that $800, and if they are down on that man and that woman as they are on me they will need it and it will save them the expense of building one. For all, that man and that woman can git off if they have a few dollars to give the man Cahalan as the Chinaman did that was in for trying to kill another man. He gave Cahalan money for not to try him and Cahalan thought it would be better than send him for two years and then he could play pool at Still Kelly's saloon and high ball at Lawrence's saloon, and he offered to get Dan Wilson out for $20. But Wilson didn't have the money. And McDonald, if he had had one hundred dollars, he would not have been here. John, this is the truth. Cahalan may doubt it, but if you see John Gates, ask him.
Henry McDonald."

The references to 'that man and that woman' imply that someone was paid to testify against him, but their testimony doesn't appear in the *Avalanche* account. The full account of the trial would be in the hands of the presiding judge and so far it has not turned up.

It is clear that he meant to damage the prosecutor's reputation in this letter. Whether his accusations were just "jailhouse gossip" or had some basis in fact we have no way of knowing.

The Boise paper of the time, the *Idaho Statesman,* carried a story of the hanging that was almost as vengeful as McDonald's letter. "The execution of McDonald at Silver City was something more than the mere slaughter of a hardened wretch to gratify the bloodthirsty desire of an excited mob. And it is probable that in all the records of capital punishment on the Pacific Coast, there never was a more callous criminal." He compares him to a man who was hung at The Dalles two years before who impressed the writer at the time as "the most brutal felon of the century," but McDonald, he says, was "if anything the cooler villain of the two." Examples of McDonald's coolness are his inquiry as the wagon he was carried in approached the cemetery where he was to be hung, if the gallows were the "hoisting works", and his reply to a comment that it was a cold day: "It would be a cold day if I got left" — meaning it would be a great disappointment to the crowd he and the sheriff drove through to start down the road toward the cemetery. The *Statesman* in Boise said that the little mining town of Silver City was "crowded as never before" with people who had come to see the hanging. "Vaqueros and drovers from Stein's [Steen's] Mountain, farmers from Boise valley, sheepherders from the Malheur, and quartz-diggers from the Owyhee range all jostled against each other on the narrow sidewalks of the crowded streets," according to the newspaper.

The *Statesman's* reporter criticized McDonald's behavior as he stood on the gallows waiting for the rope to be adjusted across the beam. "He stood as cold as marble," he said. It's hard to imagine what kind of behavior on the part of the condemned man would have satisfied the crowd and this reporter. If he had gone to the gallows weeping and lamenting his fate he would probably have been called, in another set of the cliches of the time "a miserable, cowardly, wretch." He had been in jail for a year before he was hung. The reporter for the *Avalanche* who interviewed him three days before his death described him as "pale as a ghost and emaciated." But neither his appearance nor the fact that he left a wife and child and a mother who, he said, would "take it hard" aroused any sympathy for him in the press. The *Statesman's* writer seemed to be trying to make this the story of a professional bandit who got his just desserts. From what I have read about him and from his last pathetic letter I would say that he was a very naive man and, rather than a clever criminal, a man of limited intelligence. He belonged to that rough profession of teamsters who drove for long hours on dangerous and lonely roads, and who caroused together at stations along the way. If he had been a professional bandit, he surely would not have fallen for the trap set for him in the Boise jail when he wrote the letter that gave away his strategy under the guidance of an undercover man.

Why did he end up being the only man legally hung in Owyhee County? As he said, he was a stranger in this part of the country. His victim was well known there and he was an old man. The fact that Myers was a heavy drinker was not the sort of thing that was held against men in those days. The crime may have begun in anger and have been half-accidental, in which case McDonald might have got off with manslaughter. But he had a naive belief that he could cover up his actions with the stories he told. And he was not clever enough to tell consistent stories. Another point against him was that while he was in jail in Boise he had made three attempts to escape; one of them, when he heard that his wife and child were in a town a few miles away, was successful, but he was soon recaptured. He couldn't prove that he had another confederate in the crime — the man he called Frank Kellet. We don't know what efforts were made to find the man. His stubborn insistence on the point that he was not alone in the crime probably hurt him more than it helped. If he had made a confession and shown remorse he might have ended up in the penitentiary. Perhaps, too, the temper of the times contributed to the hanging. The West was living on its reputation as "the Wild West." At the same time civilization was closing in on the mountain state of Idaho: the railroads were coming closer, life was getting tamer. The jury in McDonald's case after their one-hour and five minutes deliberation on a pretty complicated set of evidence may have been in a "hanging" mood in an effort to revive the bad old days.

The hanging itself was a brutal act. Even the *Statesman* writer acknowledged that the rope should have been adjusted over the beam before the prisoner arrived. A priest accompanied McDonald to the gallows and spoke to him for several minutes before his hands were pinioned behind him and the black cap placed over his head. In spite of the fact that he spoke to the priest and may have confessed his crime the *Statesman's* writer says that he died "fearing God no more than he did on that day that he sent poor old George Myers unheralded to his grave."

There isn't much doubt that he was guilty of murder. But the carnival atmosphere of the deed, the three hundred and some thrill-seekers who gathered about the scaffold, the people who came for miles to see it, made it a shameful, even though legal act. One thing you can't take away from McDonald: he died bravely in front of that unwholesome mob.

7

The second violent event of the eighties in Silver took place on August 2nd, 1884 when W.H. Dewey, later known as Colonel Dewey and sometimes confused with the hero of Manila Bay, and a bartender and beer brewer named Joseph Koenig exchanged shots in and around the brewery building which stood at the corner of Washington Street and Dead Man's Alley. The Alley got its name from this killing — the death of Koenig — and from two other deaths which occurred there.

The five shots heard by witnesses that afternoon furnished material for speculation in Silver for many years. One of the shots struck Koenig in the hip and he died three hours later. Because the guns used were of different caliber they made different sounds and, in addition, some were fired inside the building and some outside. Witnesses disagreed on the question of which gun was fired first, and even after two trials in Silver the arguments about the shots went on right down to the 1920s when there were still people in Silver who had heard them.

Dewey came to the Owyhees very early, missing membership in the discovery party of Michael Jordan only, according to an interview with his son in 1953[1], because of a recurrence of the malaria he contracted while crossing the Isthmus on his way to the west coast from his home state, New York. Jordan, according to the interview, had been Dewey's partner in a contracting business in San Francisco where they had amassed a small fortune. They took their profits to the Comstock where they lost nearly all of it in stock speculation and worthless mines.

His son Con told the interviewer Faith Turner who wrote it up for the magazine *Scenic Idaho* that his father gave Jordan what cash they had left after their misadventure in Virginia City to finance a trip north to look at other prospects. Jordan wintered in Walla Walla where he heard about the discoveries in Pierce in the Clearwater country and those in the Boise Basin. He joined a party in the spring enroute to the spot where Marion More's men had already staked out everything of value. He went from there to the Owyhees where he earned his niche in local history with the discovery party, but did not live to enjoy the riches found in the creek named after him. He was killed by Indians a year later. Dewey's son said that Jordan sent his father a message by a prospector returning to Nevada telling him

Morning Star Mine and Mill. Dave Fogus' house on hill at left. (Owyhee Historical Society).

about the discovery and that Dewey walked all the way from Virginia City with a pack on his back.

When he arrived, he organized other projects while his partner prospected. He built a toll road from Ruby City to the site of Silver and the War Eagle mines. He is given credit in this article for laying out the town of Silver: it was not too difficult a task considering the options in that narrow gulch. Jordan Creek makes a broad turn at the site and years of high water and constant erosion left some space to work with. On the west side of the creek there was room for two streets — one which followed the creek bank and another on a higher plane which was named Washington and became in time the main street of the town. The one along the creek was named Jordan and another one on the other side of the creek was called Morning Star after the big mine on the rocky peak on that side of town. The big white dump of waste rock from that mine still dominates photographs of Silver. It was Fogus' and More's first triumph and first disaster, financially speaking. An extension of this street to the south led up a steep slope to the first courthouse. Northward it passes the schoolhouse which is used as a museum today. In the early days it led to the Morning Star Mill farther north and an assay office of that mine which became one of the first school houses in the town. The street along the creek, Jordan, is the road that leads into town, and it is joined to Washington street by a short street, Avalanche, and further up by Dead Man's Alley. It is hard to describe the layout of such a town because nothing is really on level ground. Streets proceed for a way and then are suddenly humped by a mass of bedrock which puts the next set of buildings on a different level. A baseball diamond which was once cut out of Florida Mountain was perhaps the most level spot in town, but even that caused protests from the visiting teams from the valley because Silver's team had more practice running uphill.

At the time of the shooting, Dewey was promoting and developing mines on Florida Mountain, the huge colorful mass which forms the west wall of Silver, just as War Eagle and its spurs form the east wall. Florida had been prospected earlier but its larger veins of low grade ore were not as tempting as the obvious signs of "float" or gold and silver bearing rock on War Eagle. The ore of some of the early discoveries had been "free milling" ore; that is, it was not combined with other metals or chemicals. Much progress had been made by the time of the Florida discoveries in handling low-grade ores which required more complicated processes because they were combined with other elements. Dewey had found good silver ore at the Blackjack Mine on the north slope of Florida and he had turned up promising float at another mine, the Empire State, below it. According to a story in the *Avalanche,* his miners were taking out paying ore from the latter mine and Dewey was predicting a brilliant future for it in 1881. He was right about its worth and he was able to recoup his fortune after two expensive trials by developing and selling these mines and two others — the Blaine and the Trade Dollar. The Blaine tunnel pierced Florida Mountain all the way to another development of Dewey's at old Booneville, whose buildings he razed to create the new town of Dewey. Besides the twenty stamp mill he built there, he indulged his taste for opulence by constructing a fancy three story hotel with a cupola on top and a superintendent's house in the same style. A system of fire hydrants supposedly made the town immune to fire, but the hotel burned to the ground in July 1907. Strangely, the superintendent's house right next to it did not burn and it stood there for years looking, with its pretty light yellow paint, white trim, and Victorian carving, like a forsaken bride. Finally in the twenties it was sold for scrap and hauled away.

In 1881 the *Avalanche* reported the trial and hanging of McDonald in great detail. Dewey's first trial was reported in summary along with other district court news. The report of his second trial was also brief, but some attention was given to the oratorical powers of the lawyers and the atmosphere in the courtroom. The reason given for the changed policy toward these interesting trials was that the newspaper

The Black Jack Mine (Owyhee Historical Society).

44

had changed hands and the man who was the prosecuting attorney of Owyhee County was also the paper's editor. The write-up of the shooting and the preliminary hearing on August 9, 1884 alludes to the dual status of the editor in these words: "We make no comment upon the testimony in the case for the reason that, first, we are the prosecuting officer in the county, and second, that we do not wish to create a prejudice against or for the defendant."

The testimony of witnesses at the preliminary hearing gives some clues as to why the shooting took place. While Koenig was tending bar the night before in Sommercamp's saloon, Dewey and another man got into a fight. Koenig ordered them to stop fighting or leave the place. Dewey became abusive, calling Koenig, according to one witness "a cabbage eating son-of-a-bitch," — a reference to Koenig's German nationality. He dared Koenig to come out and fight him, saying he would "make the cabbage back out of his ass a foot long." Koenig according to witnesses did not reply. Another witness testified that Dewey had called him a "Dutch son-of-a-bitch." A man testified that Koenig had complained to him about Dewey's abuse and showed him a gun he meant to use to protect himself. Sommercamp, Koenig's employer, testified that he had come to him some time before the shooting to say that he wanted Dewey arrested to keep the peace. He said Koenig seemed afraid. On the morning of the day of the shooting, he testified, he told Koenig to make up his quarrel with Dewey. Instead, Koenig, according to the testimony of his wife and the boy who worked with him in the brewery, took his gun and practiced shooting into the woodpile behind his house.

That afternoon when Dewey came into the saloon, Koenig walked out the door, saying something to Dewey as he left. Sommercamp testified that he said: "I want to see you." None of the other witnesses heard what he said. Dewey's son said years later that Koenig asked his father to come to the brewery to taste some liquor he had there.[2] He followed the bartender to the brewery and five shots were heard from the vicinity almost immediately.

The testimony about the shots was conflicting. Some said the first shot came from the inside, some from the outside. Koenig's gun was a .38-.41 Colt pistol, Dewey's a .44 Webley. The guns made different sounds and the shots fired inside sounded different from those fired outside. A man who was first to reach Koenig's side said that he told him Dewey shot him just as he stepped over the board at the bottom of the door. A woman and her daughter who kept a boarding house nearby testified that the first shot came from the brewery. Dewey also testified that this was so. A grand jury indictment was returned against

The Trade Dollar Mine (Owyhee Historical Society).

Dewey, showing hotel and mill, near Silver City (Owyhee Historical Society).

Silver City, looking west (Idaho Historical Society).

Dewey after the hearing and in the trial that followed in September 1884 he was found guilty of manslaughter. He was sentenced to eight years at hard labor in the Idaho Penitentiary in Boise.

The man who was warden of the penitentiary at the time, Fred T. DuBois, in his book *The Making of a State* tells how the sentence was carried out. Speaking of Dewey he says: "His lawyer secured a new trial for him and as I was satisfied that he was justified in killing the man with whom he quarreled, having acted in self-defense, I treated him more as a guest than a prisoner during the four or five months he was in jail."

His second trial took place in May, 1885. From the write-up in the *Avalanche* it is plain that the shooting and the trials were a "cause celebre" in the town. Not only that, the two lawyers — R.Z. Johnson of Boise who was Dewey's lawyer, and a General Kittrell of Modesto, California who had been brought in to aid the prosecution — were well known for their powers of oratory. (I think that the California lawyer was brought in because C.M. Hays, the man who was prosecuting attorney and editor and owner of the *Avalanche,* had studied law in the office of Johnson and by bringing in an outside prosecutor the charge of collusion could not be raised between Hays and Johnson.)

"The Courthouse was packed with ladies and gentlemen eager to hear Mr. Johnson for the defense and General Kittrell for the prosecution," the *Avalanche* reports. "C.M. Hays, district attorney, opened the argument in an address to the jury of one hour and three quarters in review of the testimony, and was followed by R.Z. Johnson for the defense, who held the jury spellbound for about the same length of time with his logic and eloquence, and concluded by telling the jury that General Kittrell, who would follow him, would repay them with his eloquence for their long and patient attention. The jury was not deceived, for the first three words that fell from his lips proclaimed him an orator, not only that but a lucid and logical reasoner. [Unfortunately the writer does not tell us what those three words were.] He carried his audience with him and drew from ladies and gentlemen hot tears by his pathetic remarks and bitter invective. Indeed, we heard one gentleman say, who has listened to arguments in criminal cases for the past ten years and knows whereof he speaks, that this was the best argument he ever listened to before a jury. But with all his eloquence and lucidness as to the testimony, the jury would not look at it as he did, and as he showed it, but returned a verdict of *not guilty* [italics by the *Avalanche*] without having had time to review all the testimony in the jury room, and the defendant walked forth a free man and received the congratulations of his friend [sic]. We understand that on the first ballot eleven were for acquital and one, J.J. Conelly, for conviction, but he subsequently changed to not guilty."

Although this account tells little about the testimony in the case it does give us a clue as to why the affair continued to hold an important place in conversations in Silver for many years. Those ladies and gentlemen who were moved to "hot tears" by the prosecutor must have been surprised by the jury's speedy acquital. Even in the '20s there were hints that people had been "bought off," but there was no further litigation to support such a view.

One reason for the long standing interest in the case was that Koenig was a member of the Masonic Lodge — "a much esteemed member" — to quote an "In Memoriam" declaration in the *Avalanche* on August 16th and again on August 23rd just after the shooting. Lodges were very important institutions in Silver in this period, probably filling a need left open by the fact that there was no church in town with a resident minister and only the Catholics had regularly scheduled services. The Masons, the Odd Fellows, and the Knights of Pythias all had cemeteries near the town, and the Masonic and Odd Fellows Halls were important gathering places.

The tribute to Koenig in the newspaper stated: "Resolved that in

49

Mike Rock, with a stack of bullion (Idaho Historical Society).

the untimely death of our beloved brother Joseph Koenig the Lodge has lost a faithful and respected member of the fraternity, a true man, and society a law abiding and peaceful citizen." A month later when Dewey's first trial was held, these sentiments must have been fresh in many minds, as well as the memory of Koenig's burial in the Masonic cemetery, attended, according to the *Avalanche,* by a very large crowd.

What happened during the nine months between the two trials to bring about the jury's speedy acquital? Did some people think that Dewey had been unjustly convicted in a shooting scrape that might have gone either way? Or did some begin to reflect that what was bad for Dewey was bad for Silver because of his obvious talent for discovering mines and bringing in money to develop them? We do not know. But the case was long discussed around the stove in the Idaho Hotel. Reading about it years later one wonders not so much about the outcome as the "why" the shooting took place at all. Part of their enmity may have been due to the fact that they clashed in a saloon —a place where men made extravagant statements under the influence of liquor and felt disgraced when they lost face in front of their audience. Both men seem to have been touchy about their honor: Koenig evidently deeply resented Dewey's verbal abuse. And Dewey both before and after this event resorted to force to settle arguments. One of the antagonists he fought with on the streets of Silver at an earlier date was Mike Rock, an Irishman from County Galway, who worked with a crew of miners on contracts. They were paid by the foot as they drove tunnels or sunk shafts. Dewey's son said that his father was involved in the mine only as an overseer to measure the progress made on the contract. That resulted in the dispute between the two men. When the contract was completed Dewey was given a gold watch and a diamond stud by the Massachusetts owner of the mine. According to Mike Rock's son Tom, the miners were not paid for their contract. When the two men came to blows about it, Mike bit the diamond out of Dewy's shirt front and made off with it. When I asked Tom Rock what happened to the diamond he said: "The old man took it to New York and pawned it and sent Dewey the pawn ticket. Then he went to Ireland and married Mamma."

Three years after Dewey was acquitted in his second trial, the *Caldwell Tribune* reported this incident on August 18, 1888: "A disgraceful row occurred at Silver City on Wednesday last. W.H. Dewey, who seems to have a fondness for using his cane on other people's heads and who has had several narrow escapes, got into a quarrel with John Sullivan and struck him. Sullivan "drew his gun and fired two shots at Dewey grazing his leg but not hurting him. Dewey killed a man some time ago but was acquitted when brought to trial. Both of these men are well up in years and should be ashamed of themselves."

Dewey managed to survive his violent conflicts, recover from the financial burden of his trials, and outlive the damage to his reputation. He sold the mines he had developed around Silver and one, the Trade Dollar, was said to have brought him a million dollars. He moved out to the valley and went into railroad building. After bringing a spur line across the Snake River into Owyhee County, he had plans to bring it on up to the mines. The Blue Book was already referring to the town of Dewey as "the terminal point of the B.N.&O.R.R. railroad now under construction." But the line never crossed the mountains, ending in the sage plains at Murphy only a few miles from where it crossed the river at the little town of Guffey. Dewey had named this little town after his good friend and financial backer Senator Guffey of Pennsylvania. The Blue Book saw great promise for the future in this little town, but it was quietly merged with the sage brush around it and the bridge across the River is all that is left of the railroad spur. In the little town of Nampa, he built his grand "Dewey Palace Hotel" which he hoped to make the finest hotel west of Denver. He built it in Nampa rather than the state capital of Boise to spite some prominent men in the latter town who had reneged on a business deal. He spent his last years in the hotel. It has been torn down for some time and replaced with lesser structures. The ornate bar from the hotel can be seen at the State Historical Society in Boise. The bar and the old bridge at the site of Guffey are all that survive of the colonel's industrious efforts.

These two cases, McDonald's and Dewey's, give us an interesting glimpse of frontier justice. If they show anything in a general way about how crime was handled in those days, it might be that what you did mattered less than who you were. Suppose, for example, that the bullets from Koenig's gun had killed Dewey. Certainly Koenig would not have suffered McDonald's fate for he was well known in Silver and a respected lodge brother. But if he had been sentenced to a term in the penitentiary, it is quite unlikely that he would have been treated as a guest.

8

The anti-German sentiments attributed to Dewey by the witnesses at the preliminary hearing were probably not typical of the feelings of the rest of the town. Some of the most highly respected citizens were German born, for instance Mr. Sommercamp. The great variety of nationalities represented there made for a tolerant attitude in Silver just as it did on the Comstock as noted by Shinn[1]. From the information in the biographical section of the Blue Book and from my own recollections there were Swedes, Danes, Norwegians, Cornishmen, Austrians, Swiss, Welsh, English, Basques, Irish, Italians, and one Manxman. The risks they took working together underground and the misfortunes they often shared over delayed or absent paydays forged a bond that was stronger than national differences. But there were two groups who continued to be socially unacceptable from the early days down into the twentieth century — the Indians and the Chinese. One sign of the difference in attitude toward these two is that their real names were rarely used. Instead they were given names of English origin like John, Charlie, Pete, or Joe. In some mining camps "Charlie" was the generic name for Chinese; in others it was "John" or often "Celestial John." Indians were called Maggie, Susie, Patch-eye Johnny and so one. The *Owyhee Avalanche* followed the pattern set in other mining camp papers by using the term 'Celestials' for the Chinese and 'Lo' for the Indian. Celestials' was an ironic term for immigrants from the Celestial Kingdom or China and 'Lo' came from a poem written one hundred and ten years before the discovery of gold in California — Alexander Pope's Essay of Man.)

> Lo, the poor Indian whose untutored mind
> Sees God in clouds and hears him in the wind;
> His soul proud science never taught to stray
> Far as the solar walk or milky way,
> Yet simple nature to his hope has given
> Beyond the cloud-tipped hill an humbler heaven.

In Western newspaper language, the phrase "Lo, the poor Indian" became the code word meaning that a lot of soft-headed Easterners were showering sympathy on a bunch of lazy, but dangerous, wretches. And in a way they were right as T.R. Fehrenbach points out in his book *Comanches: the Destruction of a People*. For by the time the West (and even the Southwest that Fehrenbach was speaking of) was being settled, the Indian was no longer a threat in the East and writers there could sit back and look philosophically at the problem and decide that 'Lo' had not got a fair deal. In Idaho the Indian troubles persisted through the 1870s and it was hard to be philosophical when the arrows and bullets were still flying.

An item in the *Owyhee Avalanche* for May, 1868 was very likely written by a man who had a lot of first-hand experience with Indians — W.J. Hill, who was then the paper's owner and editor. Criticizing a story from the *Sacramento Union* which praised General Sherman for his "high-souled sympathy for the Indian and a keen appreciation of his sad condition" (quote from the *Avalanche*) the writer suggests that the general would benefit in his understanding of "Lo" if he took a trip into the interior and "had a fellow passenger killed, himself shot full of arrows and scalped, and the bloody work commenced while having a friendly (?) shake of the hand....Such outrages," the writer continues, "are being perpetrated and we are among the many who believe the perpetrators are more deserving of shot and bayonets than food and sympathy." The writer apparently wasn't aware that General Sherman had had a great deal of experience in the interior when he helped put down Indian uprisings in the Southwest. This frontier editor had formerly operated a ferry on the Owyhee River where the traffic from Nevada and California entered the Owyhees. He had been attacked and wounded many times, so many, according to the very laudatory biography in the Blue Book, that the Indians believed he led a charmed life. A contemporary, T.J. Donaldson, who once saw Hill stripped for swimming, said his body was "covered with scars of Indian arrow-heads."[2] He had also been severely wounded in the thigh by a bullet when he and others were pursuing the Indians who had murdered Jordan.

An earlier item (March 28, 1868) expressed similar sentiments:

> *Indians at Camp McDermitt* Information has been received that six Indians, some of the pet prisoners kept at Camp McDermitt all winter were allowed to depart one night last week, and in order to manifest their appreciation of the good treatment they had received, they took away with them about fifty head of stock, among which were several head of oxen belonging to Geo. Hymer of Jordan Valley who was on his way to the railroad to bring freight to this place.
>
> During the winter probably more than a hundred able bodied warriors got hungry and came in and gave themselves up at Camp McDermitt and on the Humboldt. Wonder if they will not be furnished with a good horse apiece and sent out into the mountains to murder and pillage settlers and travelers.

Another item from the *Avalanche* of the same year expresses the attitude of the time, that is, that the Indian was less than human. A dentist who had practiced in Silver had moved to Paradise Valley (a community in Nevada) where, the *Avalanche* reported, he had shot and killed a man known as "Italian Johnny." The dentist believed that the man whose complexion was dark was an Indian. He was, the paper said "nearly distracted when he saw what he had done." In other words it was nothing to shoot an Indian: shooting a white man was different.

Atrocities on both sides reinforced the attitudes of settlers and Indians for years. Just before the influx of people after the discovery of gold in Owyhee County, a massacre on Sinker Creek in 1860 had nearly wiped out an immigrant party. One of the survivors wrote up his experiences for a Tacoma, Washington newspaper which H.H. Bancroft used for the basis of his story of the affair. The party, called the Utter Party in some accounts and the Otter party in others, suffered brutal and prolonged agony at the hands of the Indians from September 13th until six weeks later when a rescue party found a pitiful remnant of survivors who had kept themselves alive by trading their last possessions, even the clothes they needed to keep warm, to wandering Indians for food, and when they had nothing else to trade they were reduced to eating the bodies of their dead companions.

In the initial attack on the train the Indians had approached them with seemingly friendly gestures and, by sign language, asked for food. The party supplied them with some and were allowed to move onto a rise in the land where they were defenseless and their cattle which they had corralled at the approach of the Indians were wandering in search of forage. There the Indians attacked and the immigrants fought back for two days and two nights. There were casualties on both sides. The immigrants decided to abandon four of their wagons and proceed with four others in hopes that the Indians would be content and preoccupied as well with the booty from the abandoned wagons. The Indians ignored the bait and continued to attack the fleeing party. In the end the only ones who escaped with their lives were four discharged soldiers who were with them in the capacity of guards and who fled, according to one survivor, with the best arms of the company, and a few who managed to hide out in the tall sagebrush and escape at night. These survivors — men, women, and children — suffered from cold, hunger and thievery of their weapons and blankets by Indians they met along the way during the six week ordeal. In their last days before rescue, a young boy who had succeeded in establishing himself as a go-between with a nearby Indian camp and the immigrants was murdered by them because one of the survivors had used the word "soldiers" in the hearing of the Indians. They took that to mean that the boy was betraying them. Finally a starving remnant of the party was found on

Nathan Dixon's grave stone.

the banks of the Owyhee River by soldiers from Fort Walla Walla who had learned of the tragedy from the few escapees who reached the fort. They were described by their rescuers as "mere living skeletons" lying beside the exhumed body of one of their number which they were preparing to eat. They had kept themselves alive for the last few days by eating the bodies of two of the children who had starved to death.

The story of this attack on immigrants in the Owyhee country and another terrible one known as the Ward massacre in Boise Valley had probably been spread by word of mouth to the early settlers of the mining towns in the mountains. There were other incidents after the discovery which must have kept the early settlers in a state of tension. In a battle at the mouth of the Bruneau River volunteers from Silver took part in a skirmish to avenge an attack on ranchers at the base of War Eagle Mountain in 1863. The Blue Book account says that the engagement sent "twenty bucks to the happy hunting ground and put a quietus on 'Indian affairs' in that locality." And the deaths of two of the discovery party, Jordan and Carroll, later that year was certainly well known. The Blue Book does not mention the death of the stage driver, Nathan Dixon, a killing by Indians which stirred the town deeply, according to a story in the *Avalanche* in May 1868.

When I was growing up in Silver in the 1920s, my sister and I had come across the old marble stones in the Pioneer Cemetery on the hill on the east side of town. They were lying flat on the ground amid the debris of wood that had once fenced them. The one that interested us most was the one with the epitaph:

NATHAN DIXON

May 23, 1868

KILLED BY INDIANS

AGED 32 years.

I did not find out who he was until thirty years later when I ran across the story of his death in a micro-film copy of the *Avalanche* for May 1868. A few sketchy facts had been furnished to the paper by a friend, J.P. Merrill. He was born in Indiana and moved to Iowa with his family. His father was thought to be still living in that state. At the time he died he was driving the stage coach on the long lonely road from Silver City to the ferry crossing on the Owyhee River. The stage was attacked at a point called Rocky Canyon between stations on the line. Dixon was killed by the first shot. J.W. Patton, who was riding in the driver's seat with him took the reins, but in trying to make a fast escape, he overturned the coach. The passengers who had been riding behind the drawn blinds spilled out of the coach. However they managed to keep their wits about them enough to return the Indians' fire and drive them off. Among the passengers was a lady who, after the fight, recovered an Indian's hat and ramrod for souvenirs. Some of the passengers on the coach are named in the story, among them Charles Peck, the discoverer of the rich body of ore that brought on the Poorman War, but the name of the lady souvenir collector is not given.

Dixon's funeral in Silver was, the *Avalanche* says, "attended by a large concourse of our people. After the coffin was lowered into the grave and the impressive words 'ashes to ashes and dust to dust' pronounced, muttered curses and oaths of vengeance, not loud but deep, against the accursed murderers fell from the lips of many who stood about the grave. Thus another mound, a monument commemorative of the savage atrocity was added to the many scattered here and there among the mountains. May he rest in peace on the sunny slope that looks toward the setting sun."

Two more stage drivers lost their lives during the later Indian troubles of 1878. George McCutchan was killed near the Owyhee River crossing and William Hemingway died from a wound he received when attacked by Indians at a ferry crossing on the Snake River.

The stage driver's job was one that called for more than mere skill in handling horses. The man who sat up in the driver's seat with the reins in his hands was a prime target for an Indian hidden behind a rock or a bush. He had to be a reliable man because he bore the responsiblity for his passengers' safety. And for all the people in these out-of-the-way places he was their link to the outside world. No wonder that the death of a driver stirred such bitter feelings in Silver. Mark Twain's account in *Roughing It* of the hero-worship the stage-coach driver inspired is exaggerated for the sake of humor, but he caught the feeling of the time — that the man who held the reins was one of nature's noblemen.

Attacks against miners and ranchers continued during these early years, reinforcing the bitter feelings against the Indian. A party of Chinese on the way to the new mines was attacked near the Owyhee River. Some accounts say the number of Chinese was one hundred, but others say it was smaller. One man is said by Bancroft to have escaped. His story was that his companions begged for their lives and assured the Indians that they were unarmed and peaceful. The bodies, all scalped, were found by other travelers.

John Hailey, one of the early historians of Idaho and a man who, as a stagecoach driver and operator of early stage lines left us a vivid account of his experiences, tells of an incident in March, 1863 — two months before the discovery of gold in Jordan Creek — involving a volunteer force from Boise Basin and their pursuit of Indians into the Owyhee Mountains.[3] The group, Hailey says, was made up of "miners, saloon-keepers, and a few sporting men," and they set out on this mission to avenge the raids Indians had been making on mining parties and ranchers, stealing horses and cattle and attacking the lines of supply to the mining towns of the Basin. The men had formed themselves into a semi-military body under the command of two of their number who were elected as "lieutenants." It is interesting that one of these men, a Lieutenant Greenwood, was a half-breed Crow Indian. Even more interesting is the fact that another member of the party known as "Mountain Jack" was a blond, blue-eyed, man who had been kidnapped by Indians years before. His ways were the ways of his captors and he had no idea who his real parents were. The backgrounds of these two men, one part Indian and the other a white who had been raised as one, played a part in the failure of the mission, for some of the other men were so "anti-Indian" that they resented the command of the half-breed and the Indian ways of the white man.

58

Hailey's history has preserved the account of T.J. Sutton who was a member of the party.

The volunteers sighted a band of Indians on the Snake River where they were swimming some horses (thought to be some of the stolen horses of settlers) across to the Owyhee side. They attacked the band and failing to halt them followed them into the mountains. Sutton believed that they eventually crossed War Eagle Mountain at some of the spots where the great discoveries were made a few months later. In fact, one of the men in this group claimed, according to Sutton, that he was responsible for the discovery party under Jordan taking off for the Owyhees from the Basin because of a piece of "silver ore" he picked up and took back with him. If it really was a piece of silver ore, it is not too likely that it would have caused much of a sensation in Boise Basin. There as in other new mining camps in the West it was gold that excited the fancy of prospectors and silver at that time was spoken of as rather a nuisance or a contaminant when found along with gold. Colonel Drew spoke of the placer gold in Jordan Creek as being less valuable because it was alloyed with silver and many a prospector in the early days on the Comstock considered the blackish ore mere waste rock in what was to become famous later as the Silver State. It seems more likely that the Owyhee discoverers simply felt that the basin was all claim-staked and they had better move on to virgin country.

The volunteers, like many others before and after them, were surprised by the harsh weather conditions in the Owyhee Mountains in March and, suffering from cold, blizzards, and meager provisions, came close to mutiny. They were also, says Sutton, "spoiling for a fight" and when an Indian camp was discovered the other side of the mountain on Jordan Creek they swooped down on the sleeping band and killed thirteen warriors, three squaws, and two children. They took two squaws prisoners in hopes of getting them to divulge the destination of the Indians who had escaped with the horses. When nothing could be learned from them, the lieutenant in charge ordered them released and left behind with two days' provisions. A member of the party known as Yankee Bob disappeared from the party after the squaws were released and the other men shortly heard two shots. When Bob returned he claimed that he had been shooting at rabbits, but the bodies of the squaws were found with bullet wounds a few days later. This incident, Sutton says, was not without "pallitating excuses because Emery (Yankee Bob) had a sister in the horrible Bruneau butchery a few years before, who suffered indignities that cannot be told in print, and in retaliation had sworn that no Bannock Indian should ever escape him alive. But after the above incident no opportunity was given him to gratify his just passion for revenge."

The party did not recapture any of the stolen horses from the Indians and the only lesson they taught them was that the white man was as prone as they were to seek revenge. Yankee Bob's execution of the squaws was not the only incidence of the troop's lack of discipline. Sutton himself led the scouting party whose instructions were to return to camp by noon of the day they set out. They returned two days later, but the news that they had located Indians on Jordan Creek saved them from censure. The half-breed Crow lieutenant did not dare exercise his authority as an officer because of the men's prejudice against his race. And the blond young man who had been raised by Indians in spite of his value to the troop because he knew the Snake (or Bannock) language and his skill in the practice of Indian warfare was constantly derided by his comrades who spoke of him as "that damn Indian" and in far less complimentary terms. Sutton says that he was "inclined to resent these insults to the endangering of his own and others lives and would certainly have done so were it not for the influence which Lieutenant Greenwood and myself acquired over him."

So the attitude of an eye for an eye went on over the years. In the uprisings of 1878 when Chief Joseph tried to unite the tribes in protest there were more Indian atrocities committed in the Snake River area of Owyhee County and the fear that the Indians might attack Silver led to the volunteer effort at South Mountain where Purdy and Studer lost their lives. When the menace of that campaign ended in securing most of the Indians on reservations, the residents of Silver had little to fear. But their attitudes toward the Indian continued to be much the same on into the twentieth century. An item from the *Avalanche* quoted by the *Boise Statesman* in 1895 describes the report of a "gentleman" who had been out in the Junipers — an uninhabited stretch of country between the Owyhee Mountains and the Duck Valley Indian Reservation: "There are hundreds of Indians in that vicinity slaughtering deer. Every creek is bordering with Indian camps, and every camp has piles of deer hides. Most of the Indians are from the Duck Valley reservation, though a number of Fort Hall bucks are also present. The deer are almost exterminated in that county — killed by hundreds for their hides — which are tanned and made into gloves by the squaws and sold for money to procure whiskey for the lousy bucks." So this evidence of the Indian's enterprise in filling the demand for native articles inspired nothing but criticism of his way of life. One of the most difficult things for the whites to understand about the Indian was that the division of labor between male and female was different from the white man's. The traditional work of the male was hunting and making war on the tribe's enemies. The females tanned hides, made them into clothing, gathered and chopped wood, and did the camp chores. Even in the 1920s in Silver, I can remember people laughing about the Indians who still came up there in the summer to pick up a little extra money by doing odd jobs. The standard joke was about the buck who went around lining up wood-cutting jobs and then brought in the squaws to work on the wood pile. This was ridiculous, people thought, because wood-cutting in their culture was the man's job. Even though a miner's wife often had to take up the squaw's role and go out and attack the wood-pile when she wanted to keep a fire all day to do the baking, it was still considered a good joke that squaws chopped wood.

Deep snow in Silver City (Owyhee Historical Society)

Stage (sled) approaching New York Summit (Owyhee Historical Society).

Deep winter snow in front of C.M. Caldwell's general store (Owyhee Historical Society).

Cutting ice near Silver City (Owyhee Historical Society).

Silver City in 1907 (Idaho Historical Society).

9

The treatment of the Chinese in Idaho followed the pattern already set by its neighboring states. Mining laws and union organizations discriminated against them, vigilantes took it upon themselves to punish them, and they were fair game for all kinds of pranks and humiliations. However they were welcomed in the Oro Fino district in the northern part of the State in the years following the discoveries there because laborers were scarce and many were needed to work long hours in the placer grounds the whites had staked out for themselves. And when the placers were considered worked out by the whites, they were glad to sell them to the thrifty Chinese who had saved their money. Sometimes the sales backfired on the sellers and the Chinese took out thousands of dollars from the supposedly worthless claims.[1] As in California, Montana, Washington, and Oregon, the Chinese had to pay a tax for the privilege of mining. In Idaho it began at four dollars a month and was quickly raised to five; in some parts of the State it was raised to six.[2] The tax was collected in Shoshone County (in North Idaho) and probably other places as well by a deputy from the sheriff's office who rode circuit on the Chinese placer miner, catching those who didn't see him coming in time to hide themselves in the woods. According to the reminiscences of one collector cited by Robert E. Wynne,[3] the 20% cut that the deputy earned from the fees could amount to seven or eight hundred dollars a month.

When miners drew up sets of rules for the newly discovered districts, they sometimes included a clause that forbade Orientals from mining there. The laws of the Oro Fino district in north Idaho of 1861 contained such a clause which excluded not only Asiatics but residents of South Pacific Islands.[4] The Burlingame Treaty of 1868 established reciprocal rights of United States and Chinese citizens allowing free immigration of the Chinese to the western states and this liberal policy resulted in hundreds of Chinese coming to seek their fortunes in the gold country. By 1882 the mood of the country had changed and Congress passed a law that stopped further immigration. It may have been the same mood that inspired a strike of miners in Silver in 1883. They won their demand to have Chinese labor excluded from the Owyhees. However, Chinese placer miners continued to work there so the victory probably had little force. That period in Silver's history — the beginning of the failure of the banks the mining industry depended on — was one of its low points and the thought of competition for the few jobs probably inspired the demand.

The Chinese were not socially acceptable in Silver except as servants. They were targets of pranks and jokes as they were in many mining communities. Sometimes the pranks turned tragic as one not very well-documented incident in Owyhee County shows. Just what happened in 1867 at a spot in the county which is still called "China Flat" is a little bit vague. Ten years after it happened Jim Perry, who claimed to be one of the participants in the adventure, told a story about it in hopes of interesting someone to put up some money to prospect at the site. According to Perry, a group of cowboys plotted to surprise a Chinese, Sam Lee, who had given up farming in the Reynolds Creek area, to try his luck at placer mining a nearby creek. He was kneeling beside the stream with his gold pan when a party of cowboys with Perry among them, lassoed him and accidentally killed him. They had at first planned to disguise themselves as Indians to give Lee a fright but decided on the lassoing when they found him bent over his task and unaware of their presence. Perry said that they buried the Chinese at the spot along with the bag of gold dust they found on him. Whether they really found a bag of gold dust and whether they buried it with him may or may not be true. It may have been a later invention of Perry's to interest investment in his project. This account is told in *Idaho Chinese Lore* by Sr. Alfreda Elsensohn whose information comes from 'an unidentified newspaper clipping.'

Most of the pranks indulged in Silver were less serious than this, although some could have been more so. A howitzer said to have been brought from Boise at the time of the Poorman War (Betty Derig: *The Chinese of Silver City*), but more likely the "cannon" which kept Silver under siege after the shooting of Marion More was fired by a bunch of boys with a pound of black powder in the direction of Chinatown where it destroyed parts of two shacks and thoroughly frightened the occupants.[5] "Teasing the Chinamen" was popular with boys looking for excitement for they knew that such behavior was not condemned at home and was, in fact, a source of amusement for adults. Cutting off a Chinese man's cue was a favorite sport of many mining camps, probably for the reason that it was a known disturbance to the equanimity of the Oriental. He wore his cue on edict from Manchu dynasty and losing it was a betrayal of his loyalty.[6]

It is hard to understand the rationale behind the persecution of the Chinese in the West for most of them were paragons of the virtues whites admired in themselves. They were thrifty, abstemious, industrious, and eager to please. Even these qualities were often turned to their disadvantage as in the popular phrase "a Chinaman can live on nothing." Because he knew how to live cheaply, he was considered unfair competition. But there was more to it than the fact that Chinese labor was competitive; he was also too strange. His clothes, his cues, his yellow skin and slant eyes, his baskets, and his abacuses did not blend well with the ways of Americans and immigrants from Europe. And his character was too imperturbable, too dignified, for the hurly-burly life of such places. The teasing was an effort to upset that dignity and make the Oriental act like other people. In addition, the Chinese came in large groups inspiring fear in those who preceded them that they would become a majority and take over the country. And nearly all the Chinese came as single men, not as heads of families who hoped to settle here. They were brought here at the expense of Chinese merchants or tongs to whom they were indebted to repay the price of their passage and the expense of getting them to the gold fields. They worked to pay off this debt and to make a stake to take back to their native villages where many of them had been poor landless peasants. Some of them worked for twenty years or more and their dogged persistence and self-denial mystified the whites as much as their other traits did. Moreover, the whites resented the fact that the wealth of their country ended up on foreign shores.

In the last few years, we have begun to hear the Chinese side of the story from immigrants and children of immigrants. Maxine Hong Kingston, in her books *The Woman Warrior* and *China Men*, gives us not only a picture of immigrant life in this country but a picture of the hopes that drove them to seek their fortunes at "Gold Mountain" — their name for California. Chinese who experienced the dreadful conditions of Angel Island Immigration Station in San Francisco where they were locked up like prisoners and treated like criminals while they waited for admission to the United States are telling their stories, and Paul Chow, the son of an immigrant is heading a movement to make Angel Island an historical museum.[7]

The number of Chinese in the Owyhee region in the 1870s is thought to have been around seven hundred. In other parts of Idaho they outnumbered whites at certain periods. In Elk City in central Idaho during the 1860s, they were the majority, and a white merchant who supplied them with goods in 1869 said that he got on well with them and that they were honest, hard-working, and always paid their bills.[8] Later in that part of the state resentment of the Orientals followed the pattern set nationally when Contress banned further immigration. At

The Potosi Mine and Mill (Owyhee Historical Society).

Pierce a brutal act took place in 1885 when a group of Chinese accused of murdering a white merchant was kidnapped and hung by a group of vigilantes while being taken to the county seat for trial.

The *Owyhee Avalanche* often joined in the game of baiting the Chinese, even on one occasion suggesting that they be sent to fight the Indians during the uprising of 1878. The loss of life of both sides, the writer maintains, could be borne with "a certain degree of composure. Neither the Indian nor the Chinamen should have been allowed to live in the same country with white people."[9] Such editorializing was no doubt partly the expression of a common feeling and partly the vogue for smart-alec journalism in mining camps. An editor of the nineties, (L.A. York) however, spoke well of them. Another pioneer, Linda O'Neill, saved her Chinese helper when she was cooking at a mine, from a crowd of angry miners who were in the act of hanging him. Further indication of a more tolerant attitude are cases cited by John Wunder in the spring edition of *Idaho Yesterdays,* 1981. Reviewing the Idaho Supreme Court's record in cases involving Chinese in the state he concludes that "the Idaho Supreme Court upheld a tradition of fundamental fairness and remained a bastion of justice for the Chinese of frontier Idaho." Some of the lower courts could probably not boast of such a record.

Chinatown in Silver was a strip of non-descript buildings along Jordan Street, south of the houses of prostitution behind the saloons, to the site of the present picnic grounds along the creek. Bits of Chinese pottery in the dust here are the only remnants of its existence. All the Chinese businesses and dwellings, except for the Joss House which was on the hill near the Potosi Mine, were located wall to wall on this strip. A Chinese Masonic Temple was the most imposing structure. I believe it survived until the late '30s when the general dismantling of Silver began. The Joss House on the southern hill flanking Long Gulch disappeared about the same time. Curious children in the '20s liked to peek in the open door at its elegant silk hangings and a sand table where prayer sticks of long dead supplicants still sprouted. Along Jordan street in the '80s and '90s there were Chinese stores, lottery rooms, gambling houses and dwellings. One merchant advertised in the Blue Book "Song Lee, Chinese Merchandise and Wood Contractor." Opium was sold in some of the gambling houses here and in Delamar. Some citizens worried about the influence of the evil Chinese on the young, but as Betty Derig points out, the examples set by the string of saloons operated by whites on Washington street (the main street of town) wasn't exactly uplifting either. However, the use of drugs by the white population occasionally surfaced as in an incident

Washington Street across from the courthouse. Note the fancy barber pole, also the lodging house with beds 25 cents and 50 cents. In the facing photo, this building has become Sing Chung Lung's store. Later, it was King Tan's store, the last Chinese in Silver City. (Idaho Historical Society).

Sing Chung Lung's store (Idaho Historical Society).

recalled by my relatives in Delamar. A young man who was being "walked" by two companions on the main street of town to cure him of an overdose of "hop" or opium fell dead in their arms.

The Chinese population of Silver in the '20s fell to a scattered few. Finally there were only three left: King Tan, a sometime merchant and man of all work who survived as the last Chinese in the town; Ah Moon, a dirty frightening old man who lived in a house on the east side of the creek which was covered on the outside with splayed ten gallon kerosene cans; and Little Dick, the cook at the hotel. King Tan was called "Pete" by nearly everyone in town except for a few purists who insisted that the generic name for a Chinese was "Charley." He was a lively, talkative, slim, clean, little man who literally danced over the rough streets as he went from door to door selling vegetables and meat. He had a store in an old saloon building but he preferred to call on his customers in the old way because, I think, it gave him a chance for social contact and to air his theories on a number of subjects. He loved to tell jokes, discuss religion, relay gossip, and to tease people. He was the very opposite of the stereotype of the imperturbable Oriental — the Celestial of the newspapers.

Ah Moon rarely spoke to anyone. He made his living cleaning outhouses and at other times kept busy at the Chinese cemetery digging up the bones of his countrymen for shipment to China. His occupations alone could have inspired the aversion people felt for him, but in addition he was terrible to look at; his greying hair hung over his moon-face under a filthy hat and his clothes carried years of grime. When he died in his little tin-can shack it was reported that the foot-deep litter on his floor — a veritable indoor kitchen midden — contained many skeletons of rats which were presumably part of his diet.

Little Dick, the cook at the hotel, was a quiet little man who rarely spoke to anyone outside the family who ran the hotel. He left Silver when the hotel closed.

In this town as in other mining towns, the Chinese led a difficult life. The ones who were able to save enough money from "Gold Mountain" to return to their homes were the fortunate ones; those who were stranded in ghost towns after their countrymen had left faced years of loneliness. "Pete" or King Tan made his adjustment by becoming a joker, a talker — his idea, perhaps, of a real American — but he must have spent many lonely hours in his bare rooms in the old saloon building.

Freighting on Main Street, Silver City (Owyhee Historical Society).

Eight horse team and freight wagons, Silver City (Owyhee Historical Society).

74

Stage time; early days in front of the Idaho Hotel, Silver City (Owyhee Historical Society).

Washington Street (the main street of Silver City) after 1901 (see power poles) but before 1917 (when the building next to the courthouse was remodeled) (Idaho Historical Society).

10

The prosperity that brought Silver to life again in the eighties and nineties lasted on a diminishing scale until 1914. The Blackjack Mine with its own little community on the steep north slope of Florida Mountain, the Trade Dollar and the Blaine on the opposite side of it, the Dewey Mine and its huge twenty stamp mill only three miles down the creek, and five miles farther down the booming town of Delamar with its mine working sixteen levels underground — all these profitable ventures furnished work for the miners and profits for the business people of Silver. The Blue Book of 1898 reflects the optimism of the period and pride in what was seen as a stable society. The businesses listed in the book include six general stores, two hardware stores, a tin shop, two meat markets, two hotels, four restaurants, eight saloons, a bakery, a shoe shop, a photography gallery, a brewery, a soda bottling works, two livery stables, a feed store, a jeweler, three blacksmith shops, a furniture store, two lumber yards, a tailor shop, three barber shops, (one of them advertised "baths a specialty") a newspaper, four lawyers, and two doctors. Unmentioned were the houses of prostitution located conveniently directly behind the saloons. About two thousand people lived in Silver at this time and stage lines connected it with the towns down the creek and with Boise Valley. Because it was the county seat of Owyhee County, court sessions and the routine business of the county brought people into town as well as providing another payroll for it.

Although the big mines of the period were on Florida Mountain, there was still quite a bit of activity on War Eagle. The big veins which had pushed their way to the very surface in some places on the mountain in the Oro Fino, Golden Chariot, Elmore, and Poorman mines must have come from some source below, but every attempt to follow them with shafts and tunnels ended in stalemate. An early lawyer and newspaper man, W.G. T'Vault, in a letter to F.V. Hayden, the famous surveyor and mapper of western mountains (Hayden sent the letter to the *Oregon Sentinel* for publication) compared the vein system on War Eagle to "the ribs of an inverted basket, and the dips and angles of each lode to the lattice work of the basket when completed." It was a good analogy, but in practice, following those dips and angles was frustrating because of faults and fractures that had occurred at different times in the mountain's geologic history. Veins appeared and

The Oro Fino Cut.

Silver City in the 1920s.

The author's home in Silver City in the 1920s.

Pack train transporting mine timbers near top of War Eagle Mountain (Owyhee Historical Society).

disappeared. And even though shafts pierced the mountain from 300 feet to 1,100 feet the big vein that had brought ore worth $4,000 a ton was never tapped again.

Most of the mines up there had closed after the bank failures of 1875. Some of them were sold at sheriff's sales to pay off debts. An English company bought the Poorman, working old veins and trying new stringers. They built a new mill down on Jordan Creek and put in an expensive aerial tram system to shoot the ore down to it. Some ore was milled but nothing like the early bonanza was found. The mine closed in 1903. The Cumberland on the Sinker side of the Mountain in the neighborhood of the old Elmore and Chariot mines opened up under the direction of another English company, and, following the usual extravagant practice, built a mill high on the mountain which stood there for many years, frequently photographed and painted by artists because of its picturesque location, until it collapsed in the late 1970s. The Blue Book painted a glowing picture of the prospects for this mine, so near the great ones of the past, but it closed a year after the book was published.

This was not by any means the end of the search for the big vein. In 1868 a man named Robbins had suggested that the way to get at the vein system of the mountain would be to tunnel under the base of it and work up through all the "ribs". Thirty years later his idea was tried by the famous mining team, the Guggenheim Brothers. They started a tunnel 2,030 feet below the old mines, on Sinker Creek. It was an excellent location for a mine because the snow problem was minimal at that altitude and access to the valley and the railroad accomplished without the need of crossing the high mountains. They equipped the mine with the latest compressors and other machinery, built boarding houses, bunk houses, and office buildings. Their 6,177 ft. tunnel encountered the vein of the Ida Elmore and they began a raise toward it. It is believed in some quarters that they were less than 150 ft. from the bottom of the old shaft when the State Mine Inspector halted work on the raise as being too dangerous to the miners.[1] The rest of their activity was described by *Bulletin No. 11* of the Idaho Bureau of Mines as "blind groping for the old shafts above." The mine closed in 1903. Their expensive effort in this spot was no doubt counterbalanced by their many successful efforts in other parts of the world. They probably hoped to duplicate here what Sutro's tunnel in Virginia City had done for the Comstock — tap the source of the whole system in depth.

In 1920 a group of men formed a company in Nampa, Idaho to try again in the Sinker Tunnel. They explored two veins for about 3600

Ruins of the first powder house (Idaho Historical Society).

feet. According to a Bureau of Mines report by Laney and Piper in 1926 they did not find workable ore. These two geologists point out that it cannot be concluded from these efforts that the lost lode does not exist. It may have been missed by only a few feet. This 1920 effort was not by any means the last one. The Delamar company tried to find some of the old veins by tunneling from a shaft at the base of the mountain on the Sinker side. This mine, the Afterthought, can be seen from the road that leads to the top of the mountain. It has been worked periodically through the years, even as recently as the fifties. In 1931 to 1933, some of the old workings on the mountain were explored again and, at the same time the Sinker tunnel was opened again in connection with them. Many of these mines are now caved in and the shafts filled with water.

In addition to the work done by organized companies on the mountain, there were many lone miners who often worked with the old methods — drilling by hand, hauling waste rock up from shafts by windlasses, clearing tunnels with wheel barrows, taking out a little ore now and then to be milled and keep them going. An eccentric character known as the "Count" in Silver, a man who exhibited the classic symptoms of paranoia, mined by himself on the Sinker side of the mountain for years. He had a number of guns and knives in his cabin with which he threatened anyone who approached his claim. He died inconveniently in the middle of winter and some of the men in Silver (my father was one of them) pulled a coffin up over the top of the mountain on a ski-sled, the men wearing "webs" or snow-shoes, and buried him in a spot he had indicated on a map he left in his cabin. The grave is marked by a large granite rock with no inscription. Another miner, a small, delicate-looking little hunchback, mined for years with only occasional help at his mine near the old Poorman. When he came to town for supplies he hoisted his pack on his humped back and, looking like a patient beast of burden, crawled back up the mountain. He looked too frail to attempt such a hike, much less carry on the demanding work of mining. Still another lone miner on the Jordan side of the mountain did what miners often dream of, — second only, of course, to making the big strike — he sold his mine to a company formed in Nampa in 1923. He had struck what looked like a promising vein up there and the old hopes rose again. The mine, the Never Sweat, went through the usual procedure of building mine buildings, a mill, a boarding house, and bunk house. The vein gave out and it closed after two years. The old miner went back to his native Denmark but soon returned to Idaho again.

There were many more mines on that mountain, some worked

The Delamar Mill in 1936.

The avalanche which just missed the Banner Mill (Owyhee Historical Society)

rather extensively by companies at different times, many others owned by miners in Silver who kept their claims by doing the required $100 worth of development every year in order to hold them, but rarely doing much beyond that. Occasionally one of them would run into a "pay streak" and take out some ore to mill at one of the still-standing but seldom-used mills.

The story of the mines on Florida followed the same pattern as the ones on War Eagle — they were rich and promising at first but at depth the veins did not hold up. In the twenty-five years that the Trade Dollar and the Delamar were milling ore, the State Mine Inspector's reports placed the value of precious metals recovered at $30,000,000. (R.R. Asher, "Geol. & Mineral Resources of the Silver City Area, 1968"). However, this geologist believes that Piper and Laney's report of 1926 which placed the figure at $23,000,000 was closer to the truth. Owyhee County led the state in the production of gold from 1903 to 1910 (Asher). In 1906, the Trade Dollar was said to be the most extensively developed mine in the state, the lowest level of the mine having been driven some 11,000 feet at a depth of 1,700 feet. Not long after that (1907) lower grade ore showed up and the vein narrowed. In 1910 the mine closed. The Blackjack which was on the same vein had also closed by this time. The Delamar Mine closed in 1913. (Asher)

From the year 1914 through the year 1975, there was little production of gold and silver from the region, although, like the efforts on War Eagle, it wasn't for lack of trying. The Banner mine up Long Gulch past the old Blaine Mill and tunnel carried on work through the twenties. Some of their buildings were swept away by an avalanche one year. Only the little donkey who pulled the muck cars lost his life in this accident. At the same time Pete Steele from Scranton, Pennsylvania worked some of the old leads to the Blaine Mine. The tunnel from this mine at one time was opened all the way to connect with the Dewey Mine and miners who worked at Dewey and lived in Silver often took this shortcut through the mountain in inclement weather. However, as the tunnel deteriorated they were sometimes blocked off by cave-ins and had to retreat. During World War I the Idawa Company mined on another vein up Long Gulch very close to Silver. The mine was called "The Silver City". It closed at the end of the war. There were other individual and corporate efforts on the mountain. The Daly brothers mined there for years. Miners took leases on the old properties, remembering a lead that might be promising if followed up. All through the twenties and thirties this sporadic kind of activity went on. Miners were eager for jobs as the market for their labor dwindled away. Sometimes promoters took advantage of them and hired crews without having the capital to meet payrolls. This practice left the miner with a grocery bill at the store and no wages for his hard work. As late as 1938, a flotation mill was put up in Delamar to mine the old dump of that very rich mine. And the final chapter (perhaps) of this region is still being written in the form of a very productive mine operating under an entirely new system on the west side of Delamar mountain.

There are many mines in the Owyhee region that I have not mentioned. Some, such as the South Mountain and Flint mines I did not include because they are accessible from more convenient points than Silver. They contributed little to the economy of the town. The number of dumps all over War Eagle Mountain attests to the numerous efforts up there. Florida as viewed from the town seems to have relatively few mines. That is because the big dumps are down the creek at Dewey, up the north side of the mountain in the case of the Blackjack and not visible from Silver, and up Long Gulch where you would see the huge dump of the Blaine-Trade Dollar almost filling the gulch. (The road is not open except for those on foot.)

It has often been said of this region that more money was spent looking for gold and silver than was made there in the good years. This is a generalization that would be hard to prove. Corporations and individuals are not required to divulge how much they spend on a project, and figuring profit and loss over the years would require reconciling the ups and downs in prices and the value of money. Millions were made here and perhaps millions spent. Most of the money that was made went out of the state: a great deal of it went out of the country. Even in the very early days, corporations like the Oregon Steamship and Navigation Company which had already profited hugely from transporting men and their goods up the Columbia to Idaho got in on the big bonanzas by furnishing capital and backing warring sides in disputes. W.H. Dewey was the only local man who became a millionaire. None of the money made did anything for the town of Silver as a town except to provide work for miners and trade for business people. The streets of the town were never improved; they were always the uncertain masses of humped bedrock that they are today. The county did spend some money on the courthouse in 1917 when it remodeled the remainder of what was called the Granite Block for county offices and put in the only cement sidewalk in town in front of the building. (The sidewalk is still there although the buildings are gone). The roads into the region, although passable, are still dirt roads maintained with a minimum of expense by the county. This is the great difference between Owyhee towns and mining towns like Virginia City,

Nevada. There the problems of transportation, although staggering at first, were solved by the construction of excellent roads and the building of railroads.

In some ways the unimproved roads have been a blessing. Silver has remained an out-of-the-way spot, not worth the bother for travelers who do not like to leave the surfaced roads. And so it has managed to keep its character: it is still a little mining town rather than a tourist trap. It has not been exploited and, although some of its buildings have been renovated, others are still going through the process of picturesque decay. Its future has been the subject of much controversy and it is quite likely that the controversy will go on and that Silver will go on being itself.

An old drilling contest stone.

Cemetery at Fairview on War Eagle Mountain (Owyhee Historical Society).

11

After the Delamar Mine closed, that town became a ghost town in a very short time. I can remember going to a funeral there in 1919 and being impressed by the empty buildings on either side of the street. Many, like the hotel, a meeting hall next to it, and the bunk house across the street, were well-painted and sturdy-looking compared to those in Silver, and the mine buildings with their distinctive wooden cupolas looked as if work had just stopped moments before. A few families still lived there and the funeral we attended had a connection with the fact that most of the houses were empty: two little boys playing in a vacant house had set a mattress afire and burned to death.

Many people had moved away from Silver when the Delamar Mine closed. Some had moved up the creek to Silver but not nearly enough to fill up the empty houses there. The only new construction in the town was the remodeling of the building adjoining the courthouse to provide more office space in 1917. The row of saloons across the street — an odd collection of false-front buildings — had been closed since 1916 when the state went dry. Further up the street, one part of the old War Eagle Hotel had fallen in and was being dismantled. This hotel like the Idaho which is still standing was a composite of buildings. The part that had fallen in was the bar-room. A two story building next to it housed the various families who owned it over the years and provided rooms for the guests. A little log structure on the end was used as an office and after the rest of the building had been torn down it served as a store-house for furniture. A pioneer of Silver said that this little house was built by James Carroll, one of the discovery party who was killed by Indians along with Michael Jordan in 1864. It may have been the first house built on the site of Silver City.

The town in the late teens and early twenties was not much different from the historical photographs of it in the nineties. Some of the older and more fragile places succumbed every winter to the load of snow on their roofs and some were torn down and carried off to mines on the mountains. But the streets were still for the most part lined with buildings wall to wall. Two long foot bridges spanned the gulch and one vehicle bridge crossed it below Dead Man's Alley. One of the foot bridges alongside the Masonic Hall which also spans the creek (it began as a sawmill which used the water power furnished by the creek) was still being used in 1936 but was torn down sometime before 1946.

89

Another foot bridge, old, high, and shaky, took off from Chinatown behind the War Eagle Hotel to the east side of town where its destination in the beginning was probably the first courthouse whose foundation stones can still be seen on the hillside. This was the building McDonald was tried in and held in jail in 1881. It burned in 1884 when a white prisoner set his bed afire to protest the indignity of being locked up with a Chinese. (According to a story in the *Idaho Daily Statesman* for December 1, 1943 based on an interview with Will Hawes, the last all-year resident of the town). This bridge was taken down in the 1920s.

In the early years of the century there were still three quartz mills within the townsite of Silver. The old Morning Star Mill stood below the present Catholic Church on the road past the schoolhouse. Some of its foundation timbers were still there when I started to school in 1917. The Morning Star Mine whose huge dump dominates the peak on that side of town still had a shaft house on it at that time. The inclined shaft of this mine pierces the peak for nearly five hundred feet and some of its levels lie under the town of Silver. The Lincoln Mill across the creek at the base of Florida Mountain was partly dismantled sometime in the '20s. The Potosi Mill on the side of the peak diagonally opposite Morning Star was the last to go. It survived until the forties. The white mine dumps, glistening with mica on the mountains and peaks around this town, testify to the intensive efforts to locate a bonanza, efforts which in late years often turned out, to use another phrase borrowed from Mexico, a "borrasca."

Two peaks on either side of Long Gulch became the site in 1885 for water tanks which were fed by ditches from springs farther up the gulch. If you look at the houses on the steep east side of town which were served by this system, you can't help wondering at the problems it must have posed for the installers to get water to them. In the first place, because of the severe winters, the pipes had to be put far underground to prevent freezing. And the masses of bed-rock you see protruding everywhere in town must have meant blasting a bed for them in many places. And there was the problem of getting enough pressure to force the water up the grades. Before 1885, the town depended on water from springs on the hillsides, a few wells, and the creek. Sr. Alfreda Elsensohn in her book *Idaho Chinese Lore* says that the Chinese of Silver carried water to householders of that time in buckets balanced on their traditional over-the-shoulder poles and that their charge for keeping water barrels filled was fifty cents a week. Some of the houses in town never took advantage of the privately-installed water system. They continued to get water from springs and wells. The schoolhouse had no water piped in and it was not wired for electricity until after 1925. The majority of houses had only cold water. The few who had the luxury of piped hot water had a tank attached to the kitchen range. Two or three had flush toilets but there was no sewage disposal system to connect them with, so I suppose most of the sewage ended up in the creek. Most houses had outdoor toilets, some connected to the house by a snow shed.

The town was fortunate in its early acquisition of electricity. In 1901 the Trade Dollar Mining Company built the first dam on the Snake River at Swan Falls. It was a very difficult undertaking. Much of the labor was done by hand with shovel and wheelbarrow. The heavy components installed were moved by steam-powered vehicles and many teams of horses. One great problem was the swift current of the river at that time, for there were no dams up the stream to cut the flow. The final closure of the dam was accomplished by consultation with an engineer from Chicago and a riverboat captain from Pittsburgh who directed the operation. A large crib was lowered into the final gap in the dam, and although the current pushed it cross-wise, it was immediately filled with tons of rock and it accomplished its purpose. (Information derived from an account by L.A. York, former publisher of the *Owyhee Avalanche* as told in *Hydro Power*, by Geo. C. Young and Frederic J. Cochrane, a publication of Idaho Power Company.) The dam furnished power for the Trade Dollar mine up Long Gulch, the Dewey, Delamar, and Blackjack mines below Silver, and several smaller mines. The town of Silver was lighted by electricity in 1901, several years before some of the towns in the valley. At the end of the 1930s, Idaho Power which had bought the power business from the Trade Dollar company, discontinued service, and removed its equipment.

Few of the houses in Silver were built solidly enough to withstand the cold. Many were built with 1 x 10 boards covered on the outside by wood siding. On the inside a layer of "house lining" — a muslin cloth material — was applied to the boards. Wall paper pasted to the cloth completed the job. Some of the humbler places used flattened tin cans for siding and newspapers or cardboard in place of wall paper. Wood was the main fuel until the twentieth century when wood cutters moved away and the supply of timber began getting low. The remodeled courthouse had a furnace after 1917 and coal was brought in by wagon and truck. Residents who had stoves with coal grates began supplementing their wood supply with coal. Miners who found themselves with time on their hands during slack periods in the mines often went out and dynamited the stumps of big trees cut off in early days and chopped up the broken pieces for fuel. A more difficult task

The Stoddard house (Terry Reilly).

but more rewarding type of wood gathering was chopping down mountain mahogony. This plant of the high desert was slow burning and it made a hot fire, leaving very little ash. The twisted limbs of this odd shrub were hard to cut and its untidy spiky growth was impossible to get at with a saw. It is extremely hard and so heavy that it will not float in water. Miners whose arm muscles had been developed by swinging a double-jack in the mines could drive an axe into the stubborn wood and have the satisfaction of knowing that the result was a supply of fuel almost equal to coal in efficiency.

Through the twenties, farmers from the valley still brought their produce to Silver and sold it from their wagons. The women of the town bought peaches and pears for canning and made jelly from plums, prunes, and berries. The hillsides close to town provided elder berries and choke-cherries, too. In winter, however, fruit and fresh vegetables were scarce.

The last butcher, Al Wassler, left Silver shortly after World War I to take a job in Boise. After that the two grocery stores and King Tan, the last Chinese to live in Silver, sold meat irregularly when it was available. Cattlemen sometimes butchered a beef and sold it by the quarter after the weather had turned cold enough to keep it. It was hung up high outside to keep it away from dogs and coyotes. The Idaho Hotel had facilities for refrigerating food. They kept ice cut from two dams in Jordan Creek south of town in a building behind the hotel. Some houses whose backs fitted against the hillsides had a tunnel off the kitchen for keeping food cool. People kept their shelves and cellars stocked with food for winter which they ordered from grocery stores in Nampa and Boise. It came in on the stage or was trucked in by men who hauled freight.

The "stage" as it was still called in the teens and twenties — even though in the summer it was a large touring car — was still the link to the "outside" that it had been in the early days. Its arrival, winter or summer, was the event of the day. The man who got the mail contract had a car or truck after World War I, horses and a stable, wagons and sleighs. It might be necessary at times during the year to use car, wagon and sleigh, on the same trip because of the variation of weather conditions between Silver and the railroad thirty miles away.

The main road from the Snake River to Owyhee towns through the '80s wound up Reynolds Creek to Jordan Creek near the town of Dewey. This is the route the discoverers took. At one time stage stations along the way provided accommodations for horses and passengers. Meals were served and horses and drivers accommodated overnight or for longer periods when the road was closed during bad weather or when Indian attacks were feared. All the early supplies for the first towns along Jordan Creek — Booneville and Ruby City — traveled this road. The Reynolds Creek area included a broad valley ideal for stock raising, and ranches along it raised and sold horses. In the 1870s a store was added to one of the large ranches and a saloon flourished in connection with it. (Marjorie Williams, *Owyhee Outpost,* April 1981) Today this region is one of those which have benefited from disuse. The trees have grown up again and it is no longer overgrazed. The road is still passable in good weather.

At the end of the century when Dewey's railroad crossed the Snake River and headed for the mountains (it didn't make it), a railroad station was built on Rabbit Creek and the little town of Murphy grew up around it. The railroad changed the pattern of travel in the Owyhees away from Reynolds Creek and toward the new little town. Stagecoaches traveled it for a few years until cars came into general use. The road did not follow the same route out of Murphy that it takes today; instead it paralleled the railroad up Rabbit Creek, wound up and down over bare foothills, plunged into Sinker Canyon, followed the stream to the junction of a branch of Sinker Creek and then ascended the grade. It was a long trip for the first cars on this narrow one-lane road. Motors heated up on the trip up the canyon and by the time they reached the steep grade radiators were boiling and the cars often stalled. Sometimes the passengers had to get out of the overheated car and put rocks behind the back wheels while the driver coaxed it on another few feet to the summit.

After World War I, Silver started on the last phase of its decline. The Western Federation of Miners had been strong there during the years when the Delamar and Dewey Mines were running. They had taken over a private house in the town and turned it into a hospital and dispensary. But when the big mines closed and the anti-union attitudes following the war depleted union ranks, the hospital closed. The last doctor to use the facilities was Dr. William Schuyler. By 1920 he had given it up and a few years later the drugstore next to the courthouse closed, too. The problem of getting medical treatment after that time was, at the very least, inconvenient and at times tragic. For a doctor to leave his practice in the winter time for a trip to Silver involved not only a long cold trip but an uncertain amount of time, for the road could be suddenly closed by heavy snow. However, some doctors made the trip in very bad weather conditions. One, Dr. Jones of Jordan Valley, Oregon sometimes made part of the trip by horseback.

In spite of the decline in mining activity, the town continued to maintain a somewhat optimistic spirit into the '30s. When mining engineers or promoters came into the town to look at claims, the old hopes rose again and the old timers who sat on the porch of the hotel would begin to talk about the mines "coming back."

The social life of Silver in its late years was centered around the people who worked in the courthouse. Dances in the Masonic and Odd Fellows Halls attracted outsiders from Murphy, and other towns including Jordan Valley, Oregon. Sometimes the only music available would be provided by Newt Chapman, a deaf fiddler. In the twenties, Lyle and Leona Eisenhart provided some good jazz on the saxophone and piano. Bob sleds, made by Lyle Eisenhart, Sr., a blacksmith, still roared through town on an iced track on winter nights. Children and young people skied on skis that were usually locally made. Men of the town relaxed over card games and mine-talk at the Idaho Hotel. Miner's wives had few distractions from the daylong task of keeping a house clean and a family fed. The physical labor involved in keeping a fire going to do the cooking and baking, heating water in boilers and kettles to do a washing, emptying the wash tubs, mending and patching worn articles, and making new clothes out of old ones was enough to exclude any problem of what to do with leisure time. But the main release from the daily monotony for them was an afternoon or evening visit at a neighbor's house. Although the weekly paper was still published until the end of the town's life as a county seat, the real news was circulated by word of mouth during visits.

Children growing up in a town like Silver would probably be called 'deprived' by today's standards. There were no man-made playgrounds, no efforts to organize play. The school board was not inundated with applications from teachers, for few would think of coming to this remote spot to spend a winter in cold and isolation. When a teacher did agree to come for a year, it was a foregone conclusion that she would not return for another term. The school texts were battered and worn, as well as being out of date. The names of the previous generations of users covered the fly leaves. But the school library (the room was the size of a large closet) had been stocked at some time with some very good books — Dickens, Hawthorne, Victor Hugo, Kipling, and a prose translation of the Iliad and the Odyssey. The State Library in Boise sent in boxes of books several times a year. For many of us, the short days of winter forced us into a reading habit that was almost an obsession.

During the summer vacation, passing the time was no problem at all, for the topography of the country provided a natural playground. The huge rocks of all sizes and shapes invited climbers and those whose imagination chose to turn them into forts, houses, ships, refuges, and hiding places. There were summits and peaks to conquer, the creek to fish and play in, wild flowers to gather. An expert on child play could not have designed a better locale. Skiing was the only sport that was traditional. Girls and boys began early with small skis and advanced to bigger ones. Nearly all of them were made by local men. When the snow came, it was usually heavy, covering rocks and bushes to such a depth that the mountains were smooth and safe to ski on. There were few accidents and serious ones were non-existent. Part of the reason was the heavy snow and the other was the nature of the skis. They were not bound to the foot like modern skis. A fall meant not a twisted knee or a broken leg but nothing more serious than a ski bobbing gaily down the hill as you picked yourself up.

Families moved away during the twenties and thirties. Businesses closed and the school became a one-room operation. Hopes for a new boom were shattered again and again. But still, miners were reluctant to leave this place where they had had faith for so long that "things would pick up." Many had claims which had to be worked on every year in order to maintain ownership. If they moved out of the region, it would be inconvenient and even impossible to come back and do the work. These claims were a dream of the future — of making it big. Another consideration was that for those who owned their homes living was cheap. On the outside they would have to pay rent and if they did not go to another mining community they could hope for little more than common labor.

In 1934, the blow that had long threatened the town became a reality: in the election of that year the citizens of the county voted to move the county seat to little upstart Murphy, the "railroad center."

12

When the mines around Silver closed between 1910 and 1914, an effort was launched in the agricultural regions of the county along the Snake River to move the county seat to a spot that would be more accessible the year round. In spite of the recent prosperity of the mines, the roads across the mountains had never been greatly improved and in the worst weather they could be impassable. Agriculture, booming from irrigation projects like the now federally-funded Arrowrock Dam on the Boise River, was replacing mining as the main industry of the southern part of the state and the towns in Owyhee County south of the Snake River were sharing in the prosperity. The problem with moving the county seat was the size of the county. Homedale, near the Oregon border, showed promise of becoming a center for farmers but two rivals east along the Snake — Bruneau and Grandview — were eighty miles from that town. The vast southern region of the county bordered by Nevada and Oregon had a few communities that were more way-stations than towns, none of which could be considered candidates for a county seat. Bruneau or Grandview would be more convenient for this part of the population than Homedale. The dilemma was not solved until 1934 when Murphy became the successful bidder for the honor.

At this time Murphy was prospering as a shipping point for livestock from the sheep and cattle ranches of the county. But just thirteen years after it won the prize of the county seat it lost the main prop of its prosperity — the railroad that Dewey had built to haul ore from his mines. When truckers began hauling livestock directly from the fields in the '40s the railroad no longer made a profit.[1] The railroad station where the stagecoach from Silver used to meet the train from Nampa was torn down and the hotel, the bar, and other businesses that had thrived from the traffic closed up shop. The new courthouse was built on a hill south of town in 1936 at a cost of $15,900. (ibid) The road from the Snake River to the courthouse bypasses the old part of town.

The choice of Murphy as a county seat was not a bad one in spite of the town's decline, for its central location between the rival towns of east and west provides an equidistant trip for both. And the ranchers in the far reaches of the southern part of the county have solved their problems by using a small landing strip in front of the courthouse for

Jim Welch and Chris Conway at work at the Oro Grande
Mine, War Eagle Mountain, 1936.

Silver City in 1936.

The schoolhouse and hotel in Delamar in 1936.

The Masonic Hall in 1936.

The old telephone office, once Knapp's Drug Store.

their private planes. Murphy's tiny population of less than fifty people makes it one of the smallest county seats in the country. A combined gas station and restaurant, the Owyhee Historical Society buildings, the post office, a title company office, and several private houses share the hillside. Several more houses are located on the hill behind the former business district.

Other towns in the county have long surpassed it in prosperity and population. Homedale is the largest town in the county with 1,739. Grandview and Bruneau have about 500 between them. Marsing near Homedale has 820. The rest of the Owyhee population of 8,241 is largely rural. The Bureau of Land Management which now has jurisdiction over the Silver City area has projected that the population of Owyhee County in 1995 will be 10,856 persons, (Silver City: Draft Environmental Impact Statement) a figure that may seem incredibly small to residents of heavily populated sections of the country.

The removal of the county seat to Murphy was catastrophic for Silver. The Idaho Hotel which had accommodated juries, judges, lawyers, and witnesses during the course of many trials closed its doors. The *Owyhee Avalanche* printed its last edition. The power company made plans to remove its equipment. The school closed in 1938. And in 1943 it ceased officially to be a town when the post office was discontinued.

In 1943, Will Hawes, son of a longtime store-keeper in Silver said goodbye to the only other full time resident, Carl Johnson, a miner, who was leaving for the outside. The scene of Carl's leave taking was photographed by the *Idaho Daily Statesman* and a long article reviewing the town's history accompanied it. The headline over the piece stated "Only One Man Stays Among Ruins of Idaho's Famous Old Silver City."[2] Articles about the "one-man town" appeared in other western newspapers. Tourists began to come in the summer months to see this unique place and along with those who came merely to look and learn were those who came to loot and vandalize. They stole gravestones. (Purdy's and Chris Studer's among others) They broke into private houses and rifled them for antiques. They broke irreplaceable stained glass windows in the Episcopal Church. The sheriff's office in Murphy deputized Will Hawes and he carried a gun which he had to use on occasion to scare off determined looters.

Some of the people who had kept their houses in Silver came back to spend vacations there but during the War few came, and at the end of it the sight that greeted returning natives was disheartening. The courthouse had been sold for scrap and torn down. The false front buildings across the street disappeared and someone even found use

Will Hawes, the "last resident" of Silver City; 1950s.

for the boards of the old footbridge across Jordan Creek. The huge iron machinery of the early day mines and mills was carted off for scrap during the war. A fire broke out in an old stone storage building and a string of houses on the hill behind it burned to the ground. The picture which accompanied the story in the *Statesman* about Will Hawes and the one-man town (Dec. 1, 1943) shows it at what must be the lowest point in its history — a ghostly deserted wreck. In 1946 when I visited it, the streets were still littered with discarded county papers, pieces of old catalogues, wall paper from vanished buildings, and shattered glass.

Some people who had grown up in the town were bitter about the disposal of the courthouse. When I asked one of them who was there for the summer why it had been torn down he said with disgust, "To make a spud cellar." (A farmer in the valley had hauled it away for use on his farm.) A few people realized that its demolition was an historic loss but it was not until interest in local history in the sixties and seventies set a higher value on the past that the enormity of it was felt. The building whose cut stone arches still stand — a Roman Forum of the early West — was the only well constructed one in town. In the days when the county building sat across the creek on the east side of town this building was known as "the Granite Block." It housed various businesses until 1884 when the old courthouse burned. The upstairs room, constructed of wood, had been a miner's meeting hall and was well known as 'Champion Hall'.[3] One interesting feature of the building even after it became the courthouse and the room above was used for a courtroom was that the upstairs could only be reached by an outside stairway: the stairs survived somehow and now ascend to empty space.

There is still enough of the town left to surprise ghost town enthusiasts who have traveled rough roads to see other formerly lively places which turned out to be two or three sagging cabins. According to the BLM's survey, there are seventy major buildings owned by sixty individuals and families. Some, like the Idaho Hotel, are complex structures made up of several buildings. A large house on the east side of the creek, the Stoddard house, stands out among the modest miners' homes. Its position on the hill, its size, and the ornate carving that adorns it, give a somewhat false impression of its importance in the town. It was not the home of a very wealthy man. The man who built it, Jack Stoddard, sold a mine to the Delamar Company and put quite a bit of money into building and furnishing this house. The carving that distinguishes it was done by Otto Patschek, a cabinet maker, whose artistry appears on other buildings in town. As for the position

The courthouse in 1936

"Stairway to nowhere" and corner of the old courthouse.

of the house on the hill, that, too, is an illusion as far as the past history of the town goes. For the hill was crowded with houses and Dewey's large white house obscured the view of this house almost completely. The front portico of the Stoddard house was the only part of it that was painted because it was the only part that was visible from below.

The schoolhouse, the Masonic Hall, the former Episcopal Church, now Catholic, the old *Avalanche* Office, a number of former stores, an undertaking parlor, the telephone office, a building which housed a doctor's office, a building used for county offices before 1917, the post office, and the Odd Fellows' Hall make up the business section of the town. The private houses are scattered up and down the rocky mountain sides.

The number of people who visit the town, including summer residents, has been estimated at twenty to thirty thousand a year by the Bureau of Land Management and the Silver City Taxpayers Association. (D.E.I.S.)[4] The Owyhee Cattlemen's Association attracts as many as one thousand to their annual meeting which features a barbecue and a dance. The Masons also hold a yearly meeting in the town. Mass is said at the Catholic Church once a year. Tour buses from the valley occasionally bring in a load of sightseers. Most of those who visit it come from the valley towns of the Boise and Snake Rivers. But people from every state and many foreign countries have also found their way to this isolated spot, according to a register kept at the Idaho Hotel. (D.E.I.S.) However many people who live within fifty miles of it have never made the trip.

Not all former residents are happy that their home town has become a tourist attraction. Some would prefer to keep it as a private summer residence for those who still own houses here and those who come back to work on the claims that still lie around and under the town. And some people who lived here in years past are so shocked at what has happened to the town that they refuse to come back and look at it in its hour of disgrace. One woman whose grandparents were pioneers of the sixties never came back to see it after the demolition of the 1940s, although she lived within twenty-five miles of it for years. Other former townspeople have taken the changes in stride, joining in efforts to uncover its history and preserve the buildings that remain. Some houses have been passed on to second, third, and even fourth generation descendents; others have been sold to newcomers.

Living in Silver in the mild summer months has many attractions but it still requires a bit of the pioneer spirit. There is no electricity.

The Hawes store, formerly Sommercamp's store (Terry Reilly).

The hotel has its own power plant and propane for heating and refrigeration. Since the town has become an historic preservation site wood-cutting is not allowed and fuel has to be brought in. The old water system is unreliable and unsafe. A group of residents is trying to raise money to remedy this situation but in the meantime it is advisable to bring drinking water along. Garbage disposal is an individual responsibility and the disposal of human waste has become a health concern unknown in former times. Mornings and evenings are very cool and those who want to conserve fuel find it convenient to go to bed early and rise late. Violent thunder storms often descend without much notice on the town making its rocky sides echo with blasts. There are still four telephones in town so vacationers don't feel completely cut off from the outside. The hotel serves light meals and accommodates overnight guests. Ed Jagels, a newcomer to the town, bought it from the estate of Tom Rock, son of pioneer Mike, in 1972. He has brought in a collection of antiques to refurbish the hotel and has made it an interesting stop for tourists. In winter, parties on snowmobiles find a warm haven here after a cold trip over New York summit or up the creek from Delamar. Parties of cross-country skiers also use the facilities.

Another attraction for visitors is the museum operated by Walt and Mildretta Adams in the schoolhouse. There are many mementoes of Silver's past, interesting old photographs, and some relics of the early mining industry on the second floor of the building — a large room that once housed the high school in Silver's prosperous days.

A camp ground along the creek south of town provides space for a few tents, campers, and small trailers. The Bureau of Land Management maintains it. It has no facilities aside from the toilets built by the Bureau. The water in the creek is not considered safe for drinking.

More changes, some welcome, some challenged, came to the town in the '70s. A 10,240 acre site which includes War Eagle and Florida Mountains and extends down the creek to Dewey was placed on the National Register of Historic Places as an Historic District in 1972. In the same year the Bureau of Land Managment, the federal agency responsible for the administration of the district, issued its "West Owyhee Unit Management Plan" which dealt with the future of the area. The plan, which is still being developed with public participation, aims to resolve through its Environmental Impact Statement the "use" problems of the area, that is, the occupancy of the sites by building owners (individual leases are the probable solution), the rights of mining claim owners (the whole townsite is claim-staked), and the rights of those who want to use the recreational resources. Many of the owners

The hotel in 1952, before renovation.

were shocked to learn that they didn't own the land their buildings stood on and that their use of it was "unauthorized." They had assumed that after years of living in this place that they enjoyed "squatters rights" at least, if not full ownership.

After much controversy, some of it heated, between residents and the Bureau the matter may be resolved by granting twenty-year leases to building owners, leases which would be renewable to heirs of the buildings; such leasing arrangements have been used for other federally controlled lands in the State. However some of the owners have indicated that they would not accept leases. Some have threatened to destroy their property rather than to go along with the leasing idea. They believe that the land should be deeded to them.

The problem is complicated by the fact that the whole area is unpatented mining land (except for one series of claims at the base of Florida Mountain, formerly the Lincoln Mill site, later purchased by Idaho Power Company and now owned by Ned Williams) and the owners of these claims have rights that must also be protected. The network of tunnels under the town was always a well-known fact, but it did not seem to be a threat to the town while the town needed the mines and the mines needed the town. Under a bill introduced by

Senator Frank Church of Idaho in September, 1980 the problem of the conflict between the rights of the building owners and the claim owners would be resolved by withdrawing the leased lands from further mineral entry and at the same time trying to protect the rights of claim owners "whenever possible." (Quote from a bill drafted for Sen. Church by the Office of the Sec. of Interior.) Some of the claim owners have access to their mines which would not conflict with the leased sites. In cases where this does not apply the bill would resolve the matter by acquiring surface rights which would prevent the disruption of the townsite. The historic area is already protected by a zoning ordinance issued by Owyhee County which requires the approval of a county planning and zoning commission for any changes in existing buildings, fences, streets, or signs, and for the demolition of old structures or the building of new ones. Repairs to buildings have to be kept in key with the historic values of the town.

Although it is generally agreed that the mines in and around Silver will not enjoy another boom, there is still the possibility that the high price of gold and silver and new methods of mining could bring development outside the historic area. Only twelve miles from Silver the Earth Resources Company is operating a very successful mine on the west side of Delamar Mountain. The company acquired a three thousand acre site which includes the old townsite of Delamar in the early 1970s. After six years of exploration and construction, work began on a huge open pit mine, now the largest silver mine of this type in the world. This new method of extracting gold and silver, like other open pit operations, changes the landscape in a drastic manner. The white dumps of waste rock from large old mines changed it, too, but an open pit alters the conformity of the mountain in a way that makes its full restoration hard to foresee. The company, however, has declared itself committed to restoring the mountain as much as possible to its original condition after the fifteen years or so which it estimates will be required to exhaust the deposit. The mine is in Owyhee County and the county benefits from the taxes it brings in. But most of the economic advantage of the industry goes to Jordan Valley, Oregon. The company built a new road to this town which supplies the mine. Most of the miners employed there live in the Oregon town.

It is not very likely that a mine of this type will be developed near Silver because of the difference in formation in the higher mountains where the metals are contained in lodes rather than being dispersed in soil areas as is the case in the Delamar region. But other new methods might make it profitable to open old mines nearby and if this happened there might be conflict over new development and historic preservation. Most residents and former residents are proud of their town's historic past, but they are not in favor of development of the town as an attraction. At a meeting of interested parties in 1974 (*Idaho Daily Statesman,* March 7, 1974) the idea of development in the form of a paved road into the town, a lodge, and scenic rides through the area was rejected by residents and BLM. An organization known as the Owyhee Foundation of Idaho had had hopes of promoting such a plan according to the *Statesman* story. It is probable that the town will survive simply as an old mining town where those who own buildings come to enjoy it and where tourists who like back country recreation find delight in new experiences.

The "Bride" stone.

13

"Silver City, Idaho Territory" was a name in the 1860s with magic connotations. Phrases like "eclipsing the Comstock", "the richest and most wonderful deposit of quartz yet discovered in the United States"[1] brought hopeful miners from near and far to share in the riches of the region. But the majority of those who came did not find sudden wealth. Instead, many took jobs in mines financed by already prosperous entrepreneurs. Some miners maintained their dreams by finding claims still unstaked which they held on to for years in hopes of uncovering the fabled riches or selling out to those who had the money to develop them.

After the financial disasters of the 1870s, the town experienced another boom in the '80s, '90s, and on into the first years of the 1900s. Rising as it did from bust to boom again, the town fostered an illusion of invincibility and the shock of the mine closures from 1910-1914 took a long time to register in the minds of the hopeful. The 1920s and '30s saw effort after effort in the pursuit of new lodes fail. But the town kept its pride of place as long as it kept the county seat of Owyhee County. When it lost that, it nearly lost its reason for being.

Even without the county seat and in the face of reckless demolition, the town did not die. Dewey, Delamar, Blackjack, Ruby City, Booneville, and Fairview have disappeared. Silver replaced Ruby City and Booneville because its location at a wide turn in Jordan Creek was better and because it was closer to the promising lodes on War Eagle Mountain. Dewey, Delamar, and Blackjack were one-mine towns. When the mine closed, they faded away. Fairview suffered a disastrous fire at a critical time in its history and was never rebuilt. As the county seat of Owyhee County, Silver lived on into the '30s. Its notoriety as a "one-man town" in the '40s forged a reputation for it as a unique and interesting place. The stimulus of a national interest in preserving historic places in the '60s and '70s came too late to save the courthouse and other historic buildings, but it saved enough to keep the character of the town.

The owners of Silver's remaining buildings have contributed much to its survival. They have shored up sagging foundations, installed metal roofs and cement block chimneys, painted and patched frail walls, repaired the damage from winter storms. Some who are unable to do the work themselves have made sacrifices to hire work done

Map 3. Silver City in 1903.

112

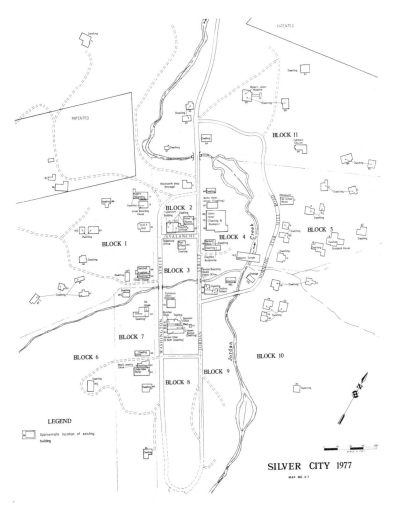

Map 4. Silver City in 1977.

113

May the old town rest in peace, guarded by the Silver City Range.

which has undoubtedly saved many of the buildings. Some of the work has not met with approval from the county commission charged with preserving the historic character of the place or with the Bureau of Land Managment. But these places are still used as summer dwellings and those who use them must make them safe and pleasant to live in. Although the goal of establishing a "recreation experience" for visitors is a laudable one, the real reason for the town's continued existence is as a summer home for new and old owners of its remaining buildings.

Physically, the town and the mountains around it have slipped back in time to the early days of its history. The remaining buildings resemble those in a very early photograph when the town was being built — frail structures along a rocky path. The mountains, fresh with new growths of timber and shrubs after years of wood-cutting had stripped them almost bare, are returning to their pristine beauty. The cover provided by the new growth has brought back the wildlife that once flourished there. On the high rocky points of the peaks you may see a golden eagle surveying the scene. As you make a sharp turn in a mountain road you may surprise a doe and a fawn at a water hole. Porcupines scramble up old mine dumps. Chipmunks and ground squirrels beg for scraps at the picnic grounds. Thrushes sing in the willows along the creek. And tiny rock wrens now make their homes in the old stones of the courthouse.

For one hundred and fifteen years this town has survived. It will probably go on for many more years, cherished by those who once lived there and those who come back every year to renew its acquaintance, providing a look at an interesting past for visitors and a new experience for outdoor enthusiasts in this remote pocket in the mountains which rise out of the desert.

NOTES

INTRODUCTION

1. Ogden, Peter Skene
   1950. Snake River Country Journals, 1824-1826. Edited by E.E. Rich. Hudson's Bay Record Society, London

1

1. York, L.A. (editor)
   1898. A Historical, Descriptive, and Commercial Directory of Owyhee County, Idaho. *Owyhee Avalanche,* Silver City, Idaho

2. Ibid.

3. Bancroft, Hubert Howe
   1890. History of the Pacific States of North America, vol. xxvi: Washington, Idaho, and Montana. The History Company, San Francisco, California

2

1. *Jacksonville Sentinel,* Jacksonville, Oregon. Microfilm copy of Drew's "Owyhee Reconnaisance," 1866

2. Richardson, Albert
   1867. Beyond the Mississippi. American Publishing Company, Hartford, Connecticut

4

1. Account based on material from H.H. Bancroft, History of Washington, Idaho, and Montana, and Merle Wells, Gold Camps and Silver Cities

2. His grave in the Idaho City cemetery is marked by a marble stone cracked across diagonally and cemented to the surface of the grave.

7

1. Turner, Faith
   1953. "Fabulous Colonel Dewey, Part I," Scenic Idaho, March-April, 1953

2. Ibid. Part II, Scenic Idaho, May-June, 1953

8

1. Shinn, Charles Howard
   1980. The Story of the Mine. University of Nevada Press, Reno (reprint of 1910 edition, D. Appleton, New York, N.Y.)

2. Donaldson, Thomas J.
   1941. Idaho of Yesterday. Caxton Printers, Caldwell, Idaho

3. Hailey, John
   1910. History of Idaho. Syms-York Publishing Company, Boise, Idaho

9

1. Elsensohn, Sr. Alfreda
   1970. Idaho Chinese Lore. Caxton Printers, Caldwell, Idaho

2. Ibid.

3. Wynne, Robert E.
   1924. "Reaction to the Chinese in the Pacific Northwest and British Columbia". Washington Historical Quarterly, XV

4. Ibid.

5. Derig, Betty
   "The Chinese of Silver City." *Idaho Yesterdays,* Journal of Id. Hist. Soc. Boise, June 23, 1978

6. Bancroft, Hubert Howe
   1888. History of Washington, Idaho, and Montana. The History Company, San Francisco, California. page 426

7. Associated Press story in the *Idaho Daily Statesman,* 1981, by Frances D'Emilio

8. Elsensohn, op. cit.

9. Derig, Betty. June 23, *Idaho Yesterdays*

10

1. Piper and Laney
   1926. Bulletin No. 12. Bureau of Mines and Geology, Moscow, Idaho

12

1. Nettleton, Helen
   1981. Murphy, *Owyhee Outpost.* Owyhee Historical Soc., April 1981

2. *Idaho Daily Statesman,* December 1, 1943

3. Interesting Buildings in Silver City, Helen Nettleton (no date)

4. D.E.I.S., for "Draft Environmental Impact Statement" B.L.M., for "Bureau of Land Management"

13

1. Richardson, Albert
   1867. Beyond the Mississippi. American Publishing Company, Hartford, Connecticut

BIBLIOGRAPHY

BOOKS

Bancroft, Hubert Howe — *History of Washington, Idaho, and Montana History of Oregon*, Vol. II The History Company, San Francisco, Ca. 1888.

Beal, Merrill D. & Wells, Merle — *History of Idaho*, Vol. 1 Historical Publishing Co., New York, N.Y., 1959.

Beard, Charles S. & Mary R. — *The New Basic History of the United States, Chapter 20*, Garden City, N.Y. 1960.

Donaldson, Thomas — *Idaho of Yesterday*, Caxton Printers, Caldwell, Id. 1941.

Dubois, Fred T. — *The Making of a State*, Eastern Publishing Co., Rexburg, Id. 1971

Elsensohn, Sr. Alfreda — *Idaho Chinese Lore*, Caxton Printers, Caldwell, Id. 1970.

French, Hiram T. — *History of Idaho*, Lewis Publishing Co., New York, N.Y. 1914.

Hailey, John — *History of Idaho*, Syms-York Publishing Co., Boise, Id. 1910.

Hawley, James H. — *History of Idaho*, S.J. Clarke, Boise, Id. 1920.

Lavender, David — *California, A Bicentennial History* Norton Pub. Co., New York, N.Y.

Ogden, Peter Skene — *Snake Country Journals, 1824-1826* Ed. by E.E. Rich. Hudson's Bay Record Society, London, 1950.

Paxson, Frederick L. — *History of the American Frontier*, Houghton Mifflin, Boston, Mass. 1924.

Richardson, Albert — *Beyond the Mississippi*, American Pub. Co., Hartford, Conn. 1867.

Shinn, Charles Howard — *The Story of the Mine*, University of Nevada Press, Reno, Nev. 1980. (Reprint of 1910 edition, D. Appleton, New York, N.Y. 1910.)

Wynne, Robert Edward — *Reaction to the Chinese in the Pacific Northwest and British Columbia: 1850-1910*, Arno Press, New York, N.Y. 1978.

York, L.A.	*A Historical, Descriptive, and Commercial Directory of Owyhee County, Idaho,* Owyhee County Avalanche, Silver City, Idaho, 1898.
Young, George & Cochrane, Fred J.	*Hydro Power,* Idaho Power Co. 1978.
Young, Otis E. Jr.	*Black Powder and Hand Steel,* University of Oklahoma Press, Norman, Okla. 1975. *Western Mining,* University of Oklahoma Press, Norman, Okla. 1970.

MAGAZINE ARTICLES AND PAMPHLETS

Idaho, A Brief History	Idaho Historical Society, Boise, ID. 1962.
Idaho Yesterdays	Idaho Historical Society, Boise, ID. 1978.
Interesting Buildings in Silver City	Helen Nettleton, Murphy, Id.
Owyhee Gleanings	Wilma Statham, Idaho Historical Society, Boise, Id.
Owyhee Outpost April 1981	*Murphy* Helen Nettleton *The Carson-Gardner Ranch* Marjorie Williams
Scenic Idaho	*The Fabulous Colonel Dewey* Part I March-April 1953: Part II May-June 1953. Faith Turner

GOVERNMENT PUBLICATIONS, STATE AND FEDERAL

Idaho Bureau of Mines and Geology	Geological and Mineral Resources of a Portion of the Silver City Region of Owyhee County, Idaho: R.R. Asher, June 1968. Pamphlet #138.
Idaho Breau of Mines and Geology	Bulletin #11: Piper and Laney, 1926.
Idaho Bureau of Mines and Geology	Bulletin #18: *Idaho's Mineral Industry, The First One Hundred Years,* 1961.
Idaho Bureau of Mines and Geology	*Gold in Idaho:* W.W. Staley. Pamphlet #68. 1946.
Idaho Bureau of Mines and Idaho Historical Society	*Bulletin #22:* Gold Camps and Silver Cities, Merle W. Wells, 1963.
United States Department of Agriculture Bureau of Land Management, Idaho State Office	*Silver City: Draft Environmental Impact Statement.* 1980.

NEWSPAPERS

Owyhee Avalanche (Also called the Idaho Avalanche at times)	Silver City, Id.

Idaho Daily Statesman	Boise, Id.
Tri-Weekly Statesman	Boise, Id.
Caldwell Tribune	Caldwell, Id.
Jacksonville Sentinel	Jacksonville, Or.
Oregon Sentinel	Salem, Or.

INDEX